Jamieson Baillie, J. R Abercromby

Walter Crighton: Or, Reminiscences of George Heriot's Hospital

Jamieson Baillie, J. R Abercromby

Walter Crighton: Or, Reminiscences of George Heriot's Hospital

ISBN/EAN: 9783337173456

Printed in Europe, USA, Canada, Australia, Japan

Cover: Foto ©ninafisch / pixelio.de

More available books at **www.hansebooks.com**

WALTER CRIGHTON:

OR

REMINISCENCES

OF

George Heriot's Hospital.

BY

JAMIESON BAILLIE.

Illustrated with Wash Drawings and Portraits by J. R. Abercromby.

EDINBURGH:
E. & S. LIVINGSTONE.

TO THE
PIOUS AND WORTHIE MEMORIE
OF
GEORGE HERIOT,
AND TO

THE AULD CALLANTS OF HERIOT'S HOSPITAL AND SCHOOLS

THIS BOOK

IS RESPECTFULLY DEDICATED.

INTRODUCTION.

GEORGE HERIOT'S HOSPITAL, Edinburgh, the scene of the following narrative, is one of the oldest and perhaps one of the most famous schools of its kind in Scotland, and, although both the Institution and its history are familiar to many, a short sketch of its Founder and his "Work," as it was called, may be assumed to be of interest to the reader.

George Heriot was born in Edinburgh, in the month of June 1563. His father was a goldsmith in that city, and was evidently a citizen of standing and substance, as it is on record that he was elected Deacon Convener of the Incorporated Trades of the city, and had represented the city in the Scottish Parliament. George Heriot followed in his father's trade of goldsmith and jeweller, and with such success that he had the honour of being, in 1597, appointed goldsmith to Anne of Denmark, the queen of King James VI., and subsequently goldsmith to the king himself. Nor did his transactions with the Court stop at the supply of jewels, for he seems to have been in the habit of lending sums of money to the king and queen as well.

When King James succeeded to the throne of Great Britain in 1603, and the Court was transferred to London, Heriot followed in its train, and he carried his prosperity with him, for in a comparatively short time, by his Scottish thrift and business talent, he amassed what was a considerable fortune in those days, the bulk of which he invested in the purchase of land in the neighbourhood of London and of Edinburgh. He was twice married, but both wives predeceased him.

He died in London on 12th February 1624, and his last Will and Testament directed that, after providing most generously for his two daughters and paying sundry legacies, the residue of his estate, amounting as it turned out to £23,625, be devoted to the erection of a hospital for "the mainetenance, reliefe, bringing upp and education " of poore, fatherlesse boyes, freemen's sonnes of the towne " of Edinburgh." Something is known of George Heriot's personality : he is known to have been a man of integrity and Christian feeling, records of some of his transactions show him to have been kindly and considerate in dealing with exacting relatives, but this scheme of his to succour and maintain the poor fatherless boys of his native city, and put them in the way of becoming capable and useful men and citizens, shows a man animated by the best instincts of patriotism and humanity.

The Trustees charged with the administration of this part of his estate were the Lord Provost, Magistrates and Council and the City Ministers of Edinburgh, and the wisdom and prudence exercised by the City Fathers during the years that have elapsed since the formation of the Trust, as well as the enormous increase in the value of the investments made, may be estimated by the fact that the revenue derived from the estate in 1897 amounted to £44,538.

An admirable site for the Hospital was secured on an eminence lying to the south of Edinburgh Castle and divided from it by the valley in which lies the Grassmarket, and the foundation stone was laid on 1st July 1628, as is recorded on one of the stone courses at the north-west corner of the building.

Progress was slow, however, and considerable interruption seems to have occurred during the erection of the building, and it was not until April 1651 that the Hospital was practically ready for occupation. It is of interest to find that at this time it was taken possession of by Cromwell and used as a hospital for his wounded soldiers after the battle of Dunbar, and to this day one of the steps in the stair at the north-west corner of the building is known as the "Drummer's step," on which tradition says one of the soldiers fell and was killed.

If there had been delay in the completion of the building no fault could be found with the manner in which the work had been carried out, and the worthy burgesses of the period must have been vastly impressed with the design and proportions of the palatial building provided for the accommodation of the "fatherlesse boyes."

A descriptive note by Mr John Begg, Architect, which appeared in the *Building News*, of 1st March 1889, may be quoted. Mr Begg says—"George Heriot's Hospital is " perhaps the greatest architectural paradox in existence. " The design is full of variety, dissimilarity of parts being " one of its characteristics; yet with such skill are these

"parts put together, that the general effect is full of
" symmetry. Then there is a large amount of mixing, or,
" rather, blending of styles, so that it is hard to say whether
" the design shows more of Gothic or of Classic influence ;
" yet the whole is so harmonious that we seem to recognise
" the guidance of one master mind through it all. And here
" appears the greatest wonder of all, for Heriot's Hospital
" seems to have been the work not of one man but of
" several men. There is a tradition, but only a tradition,
" that the original designer was the great Inigo Jones.
" This may, to a certain extent, be true, for the plan is
" known to have been supplied by Dr Walter Balcanquall,
" Dean of Rochester, a nephew of the Founder, George
" Heriot, and a personal friend of Inigo Jones. Whether
" or not this plan contained more than the merest sugges-
" tion, there is no doubt that the carrying out of the design
" and the devising all the details were left entirely to the
" Scotch master masons, William Wallace and his successor
" William Aytoun. The details, too, are quite Scotch in
" character. Begun in 1628, the building was finished in
" 1651. The plan takes the form of a square of about 160
" feet, enclosing a large paved court 92 feet square. The
" corners of the building are emphasized by four square
" towers, rising slightly above the apex of the roofs, with
" flat battlemented tops and projecting corner bartisans.
" The large tower over the entrance to the quadrangle is a
" very noble composition, and here, as also in the Chapel
" oriel on the south side of the Hospital, is shown how
" effective a blending of styles—the introduction of Gothic
" features, such as tracery, &c., into a building of Renais-
" sance character—can be made in capable hands. In fact,

"it is just this blending of Gothic and Classic, not only in
"details but in the whole design of the building, that gives
"that piquancy and originality which, combined with a
"great wealth and variety of detail, especially in the beauti-
"fully-carved ornament so lavishly spread over the building,
"makes Heriot's Hospital such a rich field of study to the
"student of architecture."

In a niche over the archway leading into the square, and on the interior elevation of the building, is a statue of the Founder in the costume of the period of James VI., and above it is the inscription, "*Corporis hæc, animi est hoc opus effigies*" [Of my body this (statue), of my mind this Work is the representation]; and here is found the origin of the name by which the Hospital was known in Edinburgh, viz., "Heriot's Work," or as abbreviated by the Herioters, "The Wark."

Sir Walter Scott, who had such a discerning eye for the interesting characters and places of his native land, has made George Heriot a prominent figure in his *Fortunes of Nigel;* and a reproduction of the statue of Heriot, with a model of the "Wark" in his left hand, fills one of the niches at the south-west angle of the famous Scott Monument in Edinburgh.

The Hospital was opened for the reception of boys in 1659, and the dress to be worn by them was prescribed by the Statutes as follows: "Their apparel shall be of sad-
"russet cloth doublets, breeches and stockings or hose,
"and gowns of the same colour, with black hats and
"strings, which they shall be bound to wear during their
"abode in the Hospital, and no other." This costume, however, was modified from time to time, and although to

the last the Herioters wore a uniform, it was neat and serviceable, though the brevity of his Eton jacket furnished the town boy with his couplet which he used to shout after the Herioter—

"Heri Heriotie
   Wi' the wee short coatie."

Primarily, the Statutes decreed that the boys be "brought up in the fear of Almighty God," and their first course of instruction was to be taught to read and write Scots distinctly and the Latin rudiments. After their education in the Hospital was completed they were to be apprenticed to some trade, the Trustees in every case making themselves parties in the apprentice indenture, and making an annual grant to each lad to assist in his maintenance during apprenticeship, amounting in all to £55 each. In the case of boys of conspicuous ability, provision was made for their being maintained at college to qualify them for one of the professions.

As years went on and the income swelled the number of boys was increased until the limit of accommodation was reached, when 180 pupils, from seven to fourteen years of age, were lodged and educated in the Institution.

Steadily the revenue of the Endowment increased, and being now much more than sufficient for the maintenance of the Hospital and its inmates, the Trustees in 1838 opened the first of a number of outdoor schools for the free education of poor children of both sexes in the City, and soon twelve of these schools were erected and equipped, providing accommodation for over 4000 children.

The attention of Parliament was, however, being directed to the whole question of Endowed Schools in Scotland, and by the operation of legislation following on the Report of the Royal Commission on such Schools, appointed in August 1882, the administration of the Trust was taken from the original Trustees; a new Board somewhat similar in character being constituted, the Hospital ceased to be a boarding establishment, and was turned into a day school. The outdoor schools were closed, and an annual payment was arranged to be made to the Edinburgh School Board for the purpose of providing free education for the children previously attending these schools. Other grants were made in aid of secondary and technical education in the city, and a large number of University bursaries open to free competition were established.

In 1886, then, after an existence of about 220 years, the so-called monastic system of residence in "The Wark" was brought to an end. Boys on the foundation are now boarded out at the expense of the Trust, living either with parents or guardians, or, failing these, with some suitable person approved by the Trustees, and they receive free education in the school as reconstructed, which is now known as George Heriot's Hospital School, and is admirably equipped and conducted as an educational and technical institution.

But with the end of the monastic system came the end of the romance of "The Wark," and the Auld Callant, as the old Herioter is called, will, within a measurable number of years, be extinct as the dodo.

The system of life under the old *régime*, when a boy spent the impressionable period between the age of seven and fourteen years, practically isolated from all outside influences, resulted in the evolution of a mode of life and thought, a code of laws and customs, and even of a dialect, which were unique, and which for good or ill divided the Herioter from life outside of his school. One result of this was to produce an intense clannishness or *esprit de corps*, and at the same time to foster an exclusiveness which effectually separated him from all outside associations to such an extent that a "Knap," as he dubbed himself, had often qualms about being seen walking with his own brother who had not the honour and privilege of being a Herioter. Nor does the influence ever die, for widely as Auld Callants may be divided in their various walks in life, the early formed bond is never broken—they are to the last Herioters; and warm, indeed, and close is the feeling of brotherhood when from time to time the gradually diminishing circle meet to commemorate their common benefactor and

> "Hail the day with grateful mirth
> That brings to mind George Heriot's birth."

While no one can doubt that the system now in operation which permits the boy to live with relatives and have all the advantages of home life, the loss of which to the child of seven was in most cases a cruelly trying ordeal, yet to the typical Auld Callant the most persistent impression of his life is that of the years he spent in "The Wark," and gifted like his fellow-men with the faculty of eliminating the bitterness of his early trials and sorrows, there remains with him always all the glamour of those wonderful years, with the memory of the long happy summer days spent in the "Greens," which seemed so spacious and so flooded with sunshine, of the winter nights when he was one of a group of wee Knaps squatted round a cosy parlour fire, and of the

"June Days" when to be a Herioter was to touch the zenith of boyish bliss and importance.

To preserve, then, in some degree, a record of a boy's life as it used to be in Heriot's Hospital is the purpose of the following story, in which an effort has been made to put in narrative form the experiences of a Herioter. In many respects his games and pastimes, his industries, even his mischief and his scrapes, were peculiar to the Wark and characteristically Heriotic, and the writer has only taxed his memory and not his imagination in the episodes through which he leads his hero and his companions.

The witnesses to these things will soon have passed away, and although the stream of George Heriot's bounty will swell and spread ever higher and wider, yet probably never again will the personal feeling of the beneficiaries for the memory of Heriot and his Work be what it was to the boys who were reared in the home which he had provided for them, and amid an atmosphere exclusively Heriotic. As an Auld Callant, therefore, apart from the pleasure of fighting his youthful battles o'er again, it appears to the writer to well become one of his sons to pay a tribute to "Geordie," whose memory is cherished by many of these "fatherlesse boyes of the freemen of the "towne of Edinburgh," to whom his motto, "I distribute "cheerfully," will be for all time a message as his life was an example.

CONTENTS.

CHAPTER I.
A Heriottie he would be—In Regimentals—First Afternoon Home—The Chapel—First Night in the School—He meets the Bully—Some o' the Connies—The Bolls—The Parlours—The Piper's Walk—The Drummer's Steps—The Shed · 1

CHAPTER II.
Friends and Playmates—First Saturday out—First Saturday Night in the Wark—The Buffie—Kids, Knaps, Cholds, and Lawds—The Garr—His First Class—Steamie in the 'Cond School—Old Meenie and her Cat—Under the Surgeon's care—Invalids enjoying themselves · · · 21

CHAPTER III.
Well again—The Bully at his tricks—The Panorama—The Food-Pot Analysed—Nabbing the Cook's Carrots—Annoying the Lawds—The Acting, Dick Turpin · · · · 34

CHAPTER IV.
The Numbers in the Square—Sixth School—Chaumont Hallowe'en—The Wark Band—An imaginary Foe—Christmas Holidays—Sword and Gun—The Return—Snow House for the Tellers—The Snow Fight of the Seventh Greens—Giving the Doctor a taste of the Weather—New-come-in-yins—Levick's Ward—Bath Night · · · · 45

CHAPTER V.
Approach of June—Lesson in Ball-making—The Friday before—June Day Morning—The Buskin'—A Happy Gathering—The Feudal Spark · · · · · 56

CHAPTER VI.
Royston—A Bathe—The Auld Bat—Skirting to Greyfriars—Nesting—A Fine Mess—The Body Snatchers—Off to Portie for a Bathe · · · · · 73

CHAPTER VII.

Rival Factions—The Spark kindled—Bat with Colinton Boys—A Court of Justice—The Knaps' Excursion—Melrose - 87

CHAPTER VIII.

The First Smoke—The Bells—Beddie's Garden Strawberries Caught—Time for reflection in the Lodge—Up again to the Wee-Dig—The Button—Applying to the Lawds for Justice - 101

CHAPTER IX.

The Exam.—Speech to the Medallist—The Vacance—Only the last Fortnight—A Sunny Day in the 'Ird Greens Roslin, a good race—A flat or a round for Innin's—A Cistern Bath, Heriot Bridge School - - - - 117

CHAPTER X.

The Return—A Crockle Scrimp o' the Cawrie—Geordie's Birthday Bush—An hour's drill with Levick—Up in the Belfry—A fight—Who did it?—Detected—An hour amongst the Pens—Well-known Rhymes—Nicknames—How they were got - - - - - 133

CHAPTER XI.

Cleek for Sel'—A Bowster Fight—Ward Stories—The King's Birthday—An auld-fashioned Bicker—A historical dog—The Auld Wife's Pig and Pear Tree—Gleedie's—The Wark Band—Recruits—Cod-ile, Cod-ile—Arrival of Carbines—Sprat-catcher the Wardsman - - - - 151

CHAPTER XII.

Winter Evenings come again—The Boar Hunt—In the Cond School—An agreeable intimation—Gossip—Quaglini's Circus—Cockie's—The Science of the Tawse—The Killing House—Simpson's—Dum, Di, Do Dum, wanting Do - - 166

CHAPTER XIII.

Hallow Fair—Concert in the Bow School—Keelies—A Fight—The Fourth Ward—Only a Lark—Fire! Fire! Fire! Astronomy with Cockie—Skating on the Square—St. Margaret's Loch—An Unfortunate Accident—Nightmare Politics - - - - - - 178

CHAPTER XIV.

A double out on the Links—Charge of the Knaps' Brigade—Fire! Fire! again—Jumping the Green Stairs—Relieve O!—Windy Friday—1st April, Hunt the Gouk—Changes—The 'Ird Ward—Not aware of the circumstances—Sandy and the Coalman - - - - - 192

CHAPTER XV.

A Putty Dive—Carpeted—An unexpected punishment—Jail-Birds—Fishing for Sock—Curious Sweets—Logie—Boot Brushing—Gleedie's Exam. in Heriot Bridge School - 206

CHAPTER XVI.

Pitt Street Baths—Barring out—Maukin'—A Dead Duck—The Escape—Robbing the Dockits—June Day—Ward Decoration - - - - 222

CHAPTER XVII.

Excursion to North Berwick—The Launch of the Life Boat—The Cricket Match—A Lawd—The last Vacance—A Bad Scrape—Very nearly a Tar—Some o' the Wifies—Fun wi' Saum'l—Feathers flying—Govies' Ward—Cutting Capers - 240

CHAPTER XVIII.

Some changes—The Dramatic Class—Rehearsal—Friday Night, the Drama—Skirting to the Pantomime—A Dangerous Climb—A Moment of Terror - - - 256

CHAPTER XIX.

Tea with Mammie—Lawds' Examination—Last Sunday—Last Night in the Wark—General Examination—Dr Bedford's Parting Words—Leaving the Wark - 268

CHAPTER XX.

After many Years - 275

GLOSSARY.

LIST OF ILLUSTRATIONS.

	PAGE
Dr Bedford	(*Frontispiece*)
The Chapel	9
The Quadrangle	11
The Kids' Bolls	14
The Shed Gate, Muscle Doo's Workshop	19
The "Wark" Bell	20
View of Hospital from Lauriston, Saturday Morning	21
The Buffie	26
'Cond School	28
Sick Room	32
Top of 'Cond School Stair	35
The "Acting"—Arithmetic Room	41
Examples from the Turning-House	44
The "Wark" Band, Old Front of Building	47
Seventh Greens	51
Levick's Ward	53
The Bath	54
A Heriot Handball	57
Mr Hunter	59
The Buskin'	62
In Greyfriars—Anderson's Tomb	76
Do. Covenanters' Prison	79
The Auld Bat	86
Lecture Room	92
Fishing Basket and Excursion Fare	100
"The Bells"	103
Shed from Terrace	108
A Heriot Button	116

	PAGE
The 'Ird Greens—A Sunny Day	124
The Cistern—Heriot Bridge School	131
Levick	136
Drill on the Terrace	138
In the Sixth School.—A Fight	144
The "Wark" Weather-Cock	150
A "Bowster" Fight—Sixth Ward	153
Mathematical Class Room—"Cockie's"	174
Fire! Fire! Fire!	185
The Lodge	199
Sandy and the Coalman	204
Confined in the Writing-School	210
"Gleedie's Exam.," Heriot Bridge School	219
Fishing for "Sock"	221
Ward Decorations	238
Ball Bottle	230
First, or Govies' Ward	253
Leaving the "Wark"	271
Bailie Tawse	273

CHAPTER I.

MRS CRIGHTON had been a widow for over three years. Her husband, a blacksmith by trade, had been in his day a hard-working man, and I daresay had left her as comfortably provided for as anyone in his position could be expected to do. A modest insurance on his life and a few pounds which the pair had managed to save between them—this was the full extent of the legacy. "The wee bit money," Mr Crighton had said, "will aye stand 'twixt you and want." That indeed was the limit of its powers. The three and a half years of her widowhood had told sadly upon Mrs Crighton's little store, supplemented as it was by her own endeavours in the way of keeping boarders. Her family was not large, but it was large enough to make no slight burden on her slender income: it consisted of three healthy, growing children—one boy and two girls. Walter was a bright little fellow of about seven, full of fun and frolic—a regular good-tempered wee chap, one of those around whom school-boys generally rally, open to fight for a friend, or play "taw" and be loser; Kate and Mary were some years older than their brother, they were quiet, homely girls, and as far as one could judge likely to turn out handsome lassies.

The children attended the one school, but as Mrs Crighton had begun to feel their fees somewhat burdensome, she was now, on the advice of a relative, endeavouring to have Walter entered on the Foundation of George Heriot's Hospital—an institution which, at the date of our story, was a free school and home for sons of burgesses of the City of Edinburgh, who, by reason of adverse circumstances, required help to bring them up and educate them. Mr Crighton, like his father before him, had been a holder of the honourable certificate of burgess-ship so that the claim of his widow was likely to be taken into favourable consideration. There were eighteen vacancies on this occasion, and, as the number of fatherless applicants was not much greater, Mrs Crighton had good hopes of succeeding with her boy. At school Walter was well advanced for a lad of his years; he could read distinctly, and was tolerably quick at figures, while, as to another consideration, he had a good constitution, and presented a robust, healthy appearance.

It would be difficult to say what were Mrs Crighton's feelings when one morning she received a circular stating that Walter had been duly elected. The document went into some detail upon various little points, but the main thing for Mrs Crighton was that her boy had been among the successful applicants, and that she was to appear with him, on a date named, in the middle of September, when he would enter, with all rights and privileges, into the "Wark."

Poor soul! her case was really necessitous; and yet, although she had been thus successful, she felt, even after all her anxious and untiring exertions, as if she could give back the circular and keep her son. Nevertheless, since the parting was to be for Walter's good and her own ultimate benefit, she resolutely resolved to bear it, hoping to make the most of her boy during the short period of holiday that remained.

As for Walter, he was perfectly jubilant at the prospect before him. There happened to be living in the locality a little "Heriottie," as the hospital boys were termed, and Walter used to fancy it would be quite grand to turn out in the neat uniform which had been made thus familiar to him. His young neighbour was always so clean and smart —in fact, a perfect band-box article, with never so much as a crease or a spot on his very exceptional attire. And then Walter had heard such stories of the good things that were to be got at Heriot's. He had heard about wondrous gymnastic erections in the grounds in the shape of ladders, swings, ropes, and poles; about grand baths, cricket, and football fields, and even about donkeys. It was, of course, all a fiction of Walter's friends, but it was a well-meant fiction intended to heighten the prospect of his going, and to make the parting from home as easy as possible. The whole thing, in any case, raised him to the seventh heaven of expectation.

Nor were Walter's sisters less delighted than Walter himself. It would be something to have a brother just like little Ross. And then how nice it would be to have him coming home on the Saturdays! And how proud they would be of him altogether! The big spotless collar, and the neat cap had a special attraction for them. Nor did they fail to think of the pleasure it would be to meet him on Saturday mornings and escort him home. Oh yes!

a great many such arrangements they would carry out when Walter was a "short-coattie."

At length the day arrived when Walter had to make his appearance at the Hospital—in other words to leave the outside world and begin a course of study in "monastics." He did not know that the place to which he was going was known by its inmates as "The Jail," otherwise he would not have got out of bed so early with the desire to be at once on the way.

Mrs Crighton went through her morning's work with a heavy heart. She knew that more than six years must elapse before she could again, as it were, call her son her own. No doubt, if he were well she would see him at home every Saturday morning; but the evening would come, and the parting would be felt as keenly as ever. Was he not her only son?

Breakfast over, and the girls off to school, Walter, dressed in his best, set out for the Hospital along with his mother.

Going from the New Town they took their way by Hanover Street and George IV. Bridge. On arriving at the gate they were met by a tall military-looking man, clad in a dark uniform and carrying himself (to use a popular phrase) "as straight as a poker."

"Ha!—h'm—new boy I suppose, mistress?"

Mrs Crighton felt as if she would sink to the ground. "Yes, sir," she answered meekly.

"H'm!—straight up by the left," and indicating the straight-up by a wave of his hand, the official stuck his thumbs into his vest pockets, and sauntered out to await other arrivals. Following the indications of the gate-keeper,

Mrs Crighton and Walter presently found themselves in the quadrangle along with one or two others on the same errand. A wardsman directed them to a room on the ground floor, where they had to wait until all had arrived.

By and bye the new boys were taken away for a dip in the bath, after which, proceeding to one of the wards, they donned the "Wark" clothes. Then, as if by some magic arrangement, eighteen brand new "knaps" or rather "kids" were turned out.

As they again reached the square, the one o'clock gun fired. Before the sound had died away there was a rising buzz of voices, and in less time than it takes to tell it, out spouted from the corner stairs a stream of boys, big and little, rushing hither and thither with the heedless gaiety of youth and animal spirits. On noticing the new boys the "Heriotties" crowded round them, quizzically scanning each newcomer with that peculiar penetration of which the school-boy enjoys the monopoly. As for the new boys they only stared in a frightened manner, clinging to their mothers like lambs to the parent ewe.

Some of the arrivals had brothers in the "Wark" who came forward with a welcome, and, perhaps, at the same time quietly pocketed the "sock" which thoughtful parents had provided for them. As for Walter, he was about the only one who had no friend to give him the hand of fellowship, and his feelings corresponded with his isolation.

One motherly woman who had been exchanging words with Mrs Crighton, recognising the state of matters, recommended Walter to her eldest boy—a lad who had already about four years' experience of the place. He spoke very kindly to Walter, whose confidence seemed to be rising;

and Mrs Crighton, who had been eyeing her son constantly, was very much relieved to see him smile at some pleasant remark made by his new friend.

The bell rang for dinner. Every boy rushed to his place in the square, the new boys following. All marched into the hall. The first meal over, the youngsters left with their parents to spend the rest of the afternoon as a holiday.

On arriving at home Walter was in a state of anxiety about the return of his sisters from school. What would they say? Would they think he looked well in his new rig-out? While he puzzled himself with these speculations his mother bustled about getting tea ready. The occasion was unusual and she was to have something grand accordingly. Just as she had finished her toastmaking and her other preparations, the girls burst in, heated and flushed with their race home, and breathless with the struggle coming upstairs, each in an effort to see Walter first. To fling their straps and books anywhere and make a dash at their brother was the work of a moment. They then hugged him and kissed him as if they were crazy.

"Oh, my!" said Kate, "how nice you look—much neater than any of the other boys who pass this way. What do you say Mary?"

"Oh, I say as you do; I never saw Wattie looking better. Let's see how many pockets you have."

With which remark Kate and her sister proceeded to count Walter's pockets; Walter presently going over them himself, by way of checking the total, found, much to his surprise, that he had become richer by fourpence.

After tea, visits were made to several of the Crightons' relatives; and what with their curiosity about Walter's pockets, Walter, when evening came, found himself the happy possessor of no less a sum than one shilling and ninepence.

As for her boy's clothes, Mrs Crighton saw that they were now of no use to him, since the next suit he would require at home would be when he was over fourteen years of age; but she folded and laid away the discarded garments, performing the duty with as much care as if Walter were to be dressed in them on the following Sunday.

It was nearly dark when they started for the Hospital, but being in plenty of time they took it easily. Arrived at the gate, Walter bade his sisters good-bye, carrying with him their promise to be in waiting for him on Saturday morning. Only his mother went up with him to the Hospital. This was the most trying time for Mrs Crighton.

As they paced slowly up the gravelled walk, the tall gaunt stained windows in front of them, showed, by the dim light burning in the Chapel, their many colours and designs. On both sides of the Chapel windows were bracketed up two bright single lamps, which appeared to stare at Walter with a questioning "What want you here?"

It was very dark and quiet; but a humming noise seemed to rise from the roof of the Chapel, which added to the peculiar feeling of dread that had taken hold of the boy.

On entering by the Govie's door and passing into the square the scene was changed. What a contrast to the quiet, dreary outside! Here all was bright and noisy, bustle and activity. Most of the windows of the wards, hall parlours, and schoolrooms were in full flare. The boys had just left their preparation classes. The hall with its steaming "pot" was ready for supper; and the youngsters were having a general scamper, indulging in vociferous lung exercise at different plays and romps. If the solitude of the outside had awed Walter, the noise and bustle inside completely bewildered him. His mother led him across the square into the parlour, where she saw some of the parents with their boys. Sitting down on one of the seats, they waited for the summons of the supper bell.

Among the newcomers were some much older than Walter, tall lads, nine and ten years of age. One, however, was about his own size — a little, chubby, round-faced, short-necked, podgy boy, who seemed to take the parting from his mother very sadly. He was in fact inconsolable, hiding his face in his mother's plaid, and crying as if his heart would break. Walter was quiet, and many an anxious glance Mrs Crighton cast at her son to see how he was taking it all. While the boys went marching into the hall, the newcomers were called out and linked on behind, their parents waiting outside. These latter taking a look through the windows, saw their boys discussing with the others their "pot" and milk. This was the cue for their departure.

And so our hero, who had never been a single night away from his mother's hearth, was left alone, a unit among a hundred and eighty of his fellows. After supper the boys were marched straight over to chapel, perhaps to keep the new ones from looking for their parents. Here the seats were mostly filled, the women servants and men belonging to the school all taking a place behind the end screens.

After an interval of a minute or so Dr Bedford floated in with the wings of his great clerical robe flying in the air. He mounted the pulpit stairs, one of the boys acting as beadle and closing the door behind him. The service was commendably short. A psalm sung, a portion of Scripture

"ABIDE WITH ME, FAST FALLS THE EVENTIDE."

read, and a short prayer, for which all knelt on the floor—that was the extent of the devotions. On leaving, one little fellow was missed; he was found still sleeping where he had, in a dead-tired condition, knelt to pray.

Walter and his companions were then conducted to their ward by Masterton the monitor. Coming out of the chapel they turned to the right, and mounting to the second storey of the south-east wing they found themselves in a large square room containing about twelve double beds and one single bed in which the monitor slept. After being introduced to their wardswoman, Maggie More, who gave them a few kindly words of welcome and initiated them into the use of the "chalker," they were tucked snugly into their beds to dream of a future paradise or otherwise.

Next morning at six o'clock Walter and his friends were roused by the cling clang of the "Wark" bell. Jumping out of bed and sleepily pulling on their trousers, they repaired to the washing-house adjoining to perform their ablutions. Every one had his own basin set into a stone table, his own towel, hair-brush and comb, &c. After they had washed themselves Maggie More busied herself among them with her flannel, giving them the finishing touches. The dressing took a great deal of time. What with new brace leathers, buttons, &c., it was rather a tedious business. When at last it was completed, the boys got seated, read a portion of Scripture, said prayers, and were ready for downstairs at a quarter to seven. The night before they had come by a private way; another, leading through the seventh ward, was pointed out to them as the one which they were to use in future.

In a day or two Walter, having had time to look about, and being initiated into a few of the simpler mysteries by his friend Ross, began to feel somewhat more at ease. He had already had practical demonstration of the word "muggin'", as also of certain other slang terms—"bat," "buffie," "gab," "lip," "jaw," and the like. But he got over these experiences without any consequences more serious than a severe reprimand in the lodge from Magnus, while from that same gentleman his antagonist got a fair "hiding" with a bunch of shoe-laces. He was very much at a loss when spoken to by some of the "knaps," but was gaining experience little by little.

"I say Murray, here's yin o' the new-come-in-yins. C'way an' we'll see what kind o' a sowl he is." This was spoken by a tall big-boned lad, with a red mark at

the side of his eye. His proper name, as that of his father before him, was John Christie. Whether as a term of endearment or otherwise I am unable to say, but he was best known as "Skin." His eye had an ugly leer over the red mark, which Walter did not like.

"Let him alane, Skin," said Murray; "it's ower sune to play ony fun wi' him yet; let the kid get his breath in the Wark first." But Skin having observed that Walter had no friend in the place likely to prove troublesome was not to be checked.

"What's yer name?" queried Skin.

"Crighton," answered Walter.

"Where do you stop?"

"New Town," was the reply, while at the same time Walter named the street.

"Has your mother got a shop?"

"No," said Walter, wondering in his own mind what business it could be of his whether she had or not.

"Ye'll no' hae ony 'sock,' 'jib,' or 'chit' and 'butt' left, have ye?"

Walter shook his head. In reality he did not understand what was said to him. Here Skin gave him a ringing slap on the side of the head, and bolted after Murray, who had already moved off.

Walter only ground his teeth, but the rising colour on his cheek told more plainly than words that when the opportunity came he would not miss his chance of returning the compliment.

Wandering out into the square, he met his friend Ross, to whom he recounted what had happened.

"Oh that's Skin," said Ross. "He's the biggest skech and meiser in the Wark. Take care o' him. Did he ask if your mother had a sock shop?"

"Well he asked me if she had a *shop*."

"Just like him, the mean beast. Whenever he finds that ony o' the new-come-in-yins have folk wi' a sock shop he makes a dautie o' them an' gets them to bring things in to him. He's an' awfu' tawnie, too; aye 'muggin' ye fur naething. I got Armstrong to gie him a pinnin' last Thursday, so I dinna think he'll middle wi' me ony mair. He's fud fur onybody if they're big enough."

Walter made no further remark, but, taking Ross by the arm, the pair went on a ranging expedition, as Ross said, "Jist to show you some o' the connies."

The first place which they came to was the "greasy pole." At one time it had evidently been a heating apparatus, but was unused for other than a coal-cellar, and, as the guide said, "for shutting knaps in to gie them a fricht." Turning their steps round under the big pillar they came to a doorway on the left.

"I ken what that is," said Walter, smiling. Ross smiled too.

"Have you been there already?" he asked.

"Yes," replied Walter. "This morning one of the boys"——

"Knaps," interposed his friend—"knaps. Mind that if ony yin o' them hears you ca'in them boys ye'll jist get laughed at an' be ca'd a sumph."

"Well, one of the knaps gave me such a lick on the leg with his hat that it felt mair like a stick than a hat."

"Aye," interrupted Ross, "that was the *number* he struck you wi'." And taking off his own cap he turned out the corner to show a little square piece of leather, stamped 164, which was his own number in the Hospital.

"Oh," said Walter, rubbing his leg, "naether wonder it was sae sair." Then he went on with his story. "So I turned round and pushed him ower. Wi' that a great lot o' them gar'd us come to the bullie, and I had a fecht with him."

"Say 'bat' when you speak about fechting, Wattie. An' did you win him?"

"No; Magnus came in an' took us baith to the lodge. I got off, but the other knap got a thrashing with the boot-laces." Here Ross had a good laugh.

"Ye'll better no say onything else but 'pints'; nane o' yer boot-laces here," was his remark.

Moving further along under the pillars, they came to the parlour door. "Were you ever up in the bolls?" said Ross.

THE KIDS' BOLLS.

"No," replied Walter. "Come on then and I'll show you them." As they made their way Walter put a question about the parlours. "That is the kids' parlour," said Ross, "an' this one on the right is the lawds'. We canna kick up ony rows there, because there's aye some o' them in readin'."

Jumping up a step or two the guide pushed open a door. And such a door! One of those thick, oaken, iron-studded doors rarely seen nowadays except in some old county prison, or on the basement flats of ancient mansions—a door, the very look of which calls up the memories and associations of a long past age of legend and chivalry.

Up they went by a high winding turret stair. On reaching the top they found themselves in a long narrow coom-ceilinged room, lined round and round with doors, and with one narrow table running up the middle. This was the boys' wardrobe. Ross opened one of the press doors, disclosing a compartment divided into three shelved spaces, each with a suit of clothes neatly folded, and a peaked cap lying on the top of them. This, so Ross informed Walter, was the kids' bolls; on the other side of the square—and here the guide pointed it out from one of the little storm windows—was a similar place for the lawds.

Walter's attention was next directed to the little turret over the chapel. Inside of that, and over the ceiling of the chapel, used to be what was called the garriers' bolls. "But they're a' shut up now. They say," continued Ross, "that once upon a time long ago the garriers got a kid up there and killed him. No mony o' the knaps have ever been in that room. Tamsin says that Meenie yince let him in by a wee door in her back room, but it's terrible dark, an' he coudna see onything."

Coming downstairs again, the boys arrived once more in the square. Ross now led Walter over to what he called "Mammie's Connie."

"Do you see that grating?" he enquired. Walter indicated that he did. "Well, there's a hole down there wi' a secret passage leading between here an' the Castle. It's what we ca' the Piper's Walk. Long long ago there was a man said he wid walk along it an' see where he could get oot, an' jist to keep himsel' cheery, as weel as to fricht away the rats, he took his bagpipes wi' him. They heard him till they coudna hear him ony longer, and he was never comin' oot at ony ither end, so efter a day or twa the garriers (nane wad gang but the garriers) went wi' plenty o' caunles and cudgels and efter gawn a long way they came on the piper, at least a' that was left o' him, an' that was jist his chanter an' some clean banes mixed wi' twa or three bits o' rags. The rats had eaten baith him an' the blether o' his pipes."

"Did they bring him out?" asked Walter.

"No likely. They turned and bolted as hard as they could and left a' thing lying as they had found it. They were a' like corpses themselves when they got back to the Wark. If you put your lug doon to the grating at nicht when a' thing's quiet ye'll hear his ghost playing the pipes yet. Sometimes he sings. Ye hear it quiet, like a soft wind—'I doot, I doot, I'll ne'er get oot.'"

Walter felt a bit "creepy" at the gruesome recital, but nevertheless determined in his own mind that some night he would put his ear on the grating and listen.

The boys now crossed over to what Ross called the "'cond school stair."

"That," said Ross, pointing to the "Govies' Connie," "is where a' the Govies gang oot an' in at, an' Bedford lives up the stair. Do you see that bell up there at the first Millar? Rare fun we have prapin' at it wi' oor baws, and when it rings, up goes some o' the warders to see what 'Beddie' wants. But we're a' oot o' the road when he comes doon again; we're aye fly enough for *that*. Come on an' I'll show you the drummer's step."

Over they went and up the stairs. A little above the second landing Walter's attention was directed to one of the steps which seemed never to have been used, while the others were well marked by the running feet.

"That," said Ross, pointing to the step, and cautiously looking round—"that's the drummer's step, and thae marks on it are his blood."

Walter certainly saw the marks, but to his mind they looked very like stains of ink, which could easily be had on that flat.

"What about it then?" asked Walter.

"Never put your foot on it" was the reply, "for if you do, every knap that sees you can gi'e you three kicks, three nips, and three dumps if he likes. I never stepped on it yet, an' I wad advise you not to. The story about that step is this:— Long ago there used to be swads in the Wark. They had a drummer for to waken them, an' when they left, the drummer jist stopped wi' the knaps. Of course there was nae bell at that time. He used to drum sae early that the knaps widna stand it, so they managed when he was stanin' on the stairs drummin' like thunder to gie him a shove, an' doon he rowed, him an' his drum. And that was the step he was killed on. So take my advice, dinna put your fit on it."

Turning downstairs, the boys went out towards the gravel. In passing through the pend gate Ross showed Walter a thing which he remarked would "pit him in a rare heat some o' thae cauld mornings." Getting up on the stone seat at one side of the passage, he ran from side to side, jumping as if he had been a kangaroo. "I can do it in four but it will take you five for a while" he said to Walter.

Then he wound up by "skinning the cat" round a bar which kept one of the halves of the pend gate closed.

Going outside, before them lay the greens—the "'ird greens" Ross called them. Turning to the left, they made for the shed. In passing along they came to a flight of steps leading from the terrace to the greens. "Can you jump?" asked Walter's friend.

"Where? Down these steps?"

"Yes, we've sometimes rare fun at 'follow the lead.' Beginning at the lowest, we jump one after the other. There's some rare birsy yins, five-five, one-nine, and twa-eight. I can manage six four, and when there's deep snaw on the ground I can do a' the stairs, an' that's a good jump. I've seen Fairbairn do a' the stairs, but no mony try't." Here Ross exhibited his six-four; but Walter thought it safer to walk down and finish with a four jump.

They now came to the shed, a long playground roofed in with sheet iron, supported on a wall at one side and by iron pillars and railings at the other. The floor was asphalted and a long bench ran up the side next the wall, on which a rest was very acceptable after a game at "Scotch and English."

"Do you see that hoose?" asked Ross, pointing through between the railings. "That's the turning-hoose where the knaps are learned what they ca' mechanics. There's a' kinds o' tools and benches, an' a lot o' turnin' laithes. The knaps make quaichs, boxes, tables and different kinds o' things in there. Sometimes we gang doon an' caw the laithes for some o' the lawds when they're ower lazy to do it for thersels an' then maybe ye get a' tee-totum fur daen it. Ower there, that's Beddie's green, where some o' the knaps gang at nichts and nab strawberries, or turnips, or carrots and rhubarb. We have rare feeds sometimes! That's Muscle Doo's workshop over there."

"And who is Muscle Doo?" interrogated Walter.

"Did you never hear o' him?" said Ross in a tone of surprise. "I thought everybody kent Muscle. He is aye on the dodge wi' his fit-rule an' his glue-pat and a lump o' wud, hammerin' nails here and there, an' aye on the grummel."

THE SHED GATE.

At this point the bell rang for "chit and milk," and the two lads made for the square, where they fell into their places. While they were standing, Walter noticed a commotion going on further up the line. A game of scuddie was in progress—a very serious matter if your hand did not happen to be in position. However, Magnus soon put an end to the sport with his usual call of "U-Re, Right face! forward!" Ross whispered to Walter to keep his half dose; and when they got out of the hall asked him to come up to the top of the sixth school stair, as he had a private box in which he kept a pot of syrup. Walter gladly accompanied his young chum, and seating themselves on the top landing the pair had a glorious "chip-in."

VIEW OF HOSPITAL FROM LAURISTON.

CHAPTER II.

NEXT day, being Saturday, Walter was looking forward with delight to the prospect of getting home to see his mother and sisters, who, on their part, were doubtless counting the minutes till they should meet again. Morning came, and the bell roused Walter as it had now done for three mornings. To-day there was somehow or other no hesitation about jumping out of bed. His little chums too appeared to be extra lively. For Walter had now learned some of his friends' names, and felt more at home with them. There was Simpson, his bed-fellow; there were Sibbald, Sinclair, Goldie, Russell, Glass, Toby Heywood, and others. Their lessons not being at first too arduous they had plenty of time to get acquainted, and they spent many a happy hour together which Walter never forgot. This morning they were all ready and eager to be out. So, after the learning and breakfast, they hurried off to get themselves ready for the road. Once more it was "U-re, Right face! Forward!" and away scurried some one hundred and eighty kids, knaps, cholds, and lawds down to the gate for the day's outing.

Walter's sisters, it is needless to say, had not forgotten their promise. Here they were at the gate eagerly scanning every face until at length they caught sight of Walter and Ross coming out in company. Once together the four made all possible haste homewards, Ross promising to call and take Walter out for a stroll in the afternoon. It was indeed a happy meeting at the Crighton home. Mrs Crighton was delighted to see Walter so cheerful. As for Walter, he was full of praise for his friend Ross; and as Ross was coming up in the afternoon, a high tea was at once agreed on. His kindness to Walter, especially in the latter's lonely circumstances, was not to go unrewarded.

In the course of the forenoon, Walter's sisters had him out amongst his old school-fellows. The result was somewhat curious. Short as had been his sojourn in the "Wark," he had already become imbued with the exclusive idea which separated all boys into two classes, viz., Herioters or knaps as they called themselves, and non-Herioters, who were dubbed keelies or hawkers, and for a knap to be seen on a Saturday or other holiday in company with a keelie or a hawker meant defilement to the Heriotic body politic, and consequent loss of caste to the offending individual, so that Walter appeared to be rather shy of some of his friends who had been his constant playmates only a week before.

Ross arrived in the afternoon, and was warmly welcomed by Mrs Crighton and her daughters. The tea party having gone off all right, Ross kept them all laughing heartily at some of his stories of the place in which they had now good reason to be specially interested. Walter had already recounted some of his week's experiences, conveniently forgetting of course all about the "buffie" incident.

The party broke up, and Walter and his friend took their walk out by way of the Canal. In the course of their stroll along the banks Ross gave his young friend a great deal of good advice, which was eagerly listened to and stored up in Walter's memory.

The walk over, it was time for the "Heriottie" to be starting "Warkwards," and after stowing some "chit" and "butt" into his pockets, the family again conducted their younger member to his palatial residence, sundry purchases being made at some of the shops on the way up.

Arrived once more at the gate, there was a renewal of promises for next Saturday, and it was even suggested that, if they could be spared, Kate and Mary should come to Greyfriars Church which the Herioters attended on the morrow. The good-byes were said, and with some affectionate injunctions from his mother to behave himself and attend to his teachers, Walter again made his way up to the "Wark."

On reaching the square, he found a number of the knaps there before him; but their behaviour was assuringly quiet. A gloomy darkness was over all, the square being lit up by only two lamps placed in the second and sixth school stairs. There were indeed four lamps, one on each stair, with large reflectors inside; but usually no more than two were lit on Saturday nights. The knaps were gathered in knots or walking soberly arm in arm round the square, perhaps five or six in a row talking, very likely discussing the day's doings and adventures. Occasionally some itinerant dealer in sweets would be heard proclaiming his wares: "Wha'll buy sock! Katie flips, six a maik!" Trade was not brisk on Saturday nights, most of the likely purchasers having been supplied before coming in. Nevertheless he persevered with his lusty cries, and generally sold something. Perhaps a member of some ruined firm would find himself in funds through one or two of his debtors (bad payers) coming forward and paying twenty shillings in the pound; and having given up business he would speculate with the unexpected cash, getting perhaps eight pieces for the "ready."

If, however, trash was at a premium on Saturday night and the sock was kept till Monday it would fetch its price.

Walter, being very tired, was glad to get cuddled down beside his bed-fellow, where he was soon in the land of dreams.

On Sunday mornings, the boys had always an hour longer in bed. Chapel and breakfast came as usual. During the morning all attended their separate classes for Bible lessons; and after giving themselves the necessary preparation in the way of extra tidiness, they were marched off to Greyfriars Church, where they occupied a gallery by themselves facing the preacher. Wardsmen and monitors were scattered about amongst the boys to preserve order, and one of the teachers was always in attendance. Dr Bedford's pew was the first one on the left; the house servants' behind.

Amongst the knaps, "sock" was in general use instead of snuff, to counteract the drowsy influence of the service. Nearly every boy had his share, some boys more, some less. Indeed, as much was often eaten in that gallery on a Sunday forenoon as would have given a fair start to a small confectionery establishment. For dinner the boys had "plum pud," that being Sunday fare once a month. Each boy got for his portion a piece for all the world like the lith of a gigantic orange. The quantity almost took Walter's breath away: in fact, to tell the truth, he wondered how many days' dinners it was meant to serve. Nevertheless, the plates were all cleared. With a full stomach and a big pocket, not a few of the boys had the audacity to smuggle away lumps of the pudding in view of the afternoon service, just to keep themselves cheery during the sermon. In some of the back seats it did not require any great exercise of sleight-of-hand to enable them to go in for extensive cramming in that way.

After tea, or rather "chit and milk," an hour or two was spent in walking about in the greens or sitting in the school-rooms and parlours, where several books and tracts of a religious character were spread about for the use of the boys. Another hour of Catechism and Bible lesson exhausted the regular routine for Sundays.

After Walter had been a week or two in the "Wark," he had made himself tolerably familiar with the words and the phrases, the names and the grades of his fellows. He knew he was only a kid; that as such he must remain for six months, performing during that time some of the lighter scogieing jobs for the knaps. At the end of the six months he would be a knap himself. That grade would last for about five years. What a stretch of time to look forward to! He would have to mount up step by step till he was past Mammie's "connie," when but one year of his time would be left. His title then would be chold, and he would hold for six months a secondary power. A chold could put any knap or kid out of his greens for any length of time which the misdemeanour of the said knap or kid might seem to merit. He had also a prior right to skech or cadge. Moreover, he could, if occasion required it, command any of his lesser fellows to "cleek sel'," or in fact to scogie in general.

After the six months of secondary power had passed, he would stand in the highest position, namely, that of a lawd. Then his power would be unlimited. Not only could he deprive his defaulters of the use of their greens but also of the school-rooms, allowing them only the square

"A MUGGIN'."

and one of the parlours in which to spend their leisure time. Nor could he do this solely on account of any grievance perpetrated against his own authority. Upon the application of any of his minor friends or dauties, he, after giving due consideration to such application (which the lawd seldom did), could pronounce sentence of confinement for any time to square and parlour, and could order the performance of almost any duty he thought fit. Should the culprit contravene, he was called into the basement flat of the North-East Wing, and was there made to suffer an additional penalty in the shape of a "muggin'."

The Lawd Government generally, although not always, included the Garr in their organisation.

> And head o' a' there was the Garr,
> In ither words the god o' war;
> Gab at his highness if ye daur,
> Doon to the buffie;
> Button up your jacket, face the star,
> Then into cuffie.

The garrs mostly had a quiet time of it. No one cared to meddle with their peace of mind; but as a matter of fact the garrs were less to be feared than some of the tawnying kind, who had neither the pluck nor the ability to fight anyone unless it were some very little knap. As a rule the garrs were manly fellows who seldom used their despotic powers except for some good purpose. Many of the lawds were of the same class. Occasionally, however, there *was* some sneaking, greedy, soulless tawnie among the lawds who made life a burden for the little fellows. To this class Walter's chastiser, Skin, made high promise of belonging.

But to return to Walter. He was getting on remarkably well with his lessons. His class was held in the Museum, a schoolroom fitted all round with cases of minerals and fossils. A large box containing an electrical machine, celestial and terrestrial globes, a writing table and half a dozen forms practically completed its furnishings. The teacher was known familiarly as the "Big Boy." Walter never learned his proper name. His instruction was for the most part of a very elementary kind, in fact, just what Walter had got at school when he was six years of age. Walter's term with the "Big Boy" was therefore comfortable enough. The teacher occasionally sent a substitute who was said to be his brother, and who, in any case, was nicknamed the "Wee Boy."

In passing in and out to his class, Walter had to go through the 'cond school, where a class was taught by one Steamie. Steamie knew the knaps, every one of them. He was an auld callant himself; and you would now and

STEAMIE—'COND SCHOOL.

again see him walking up and down the room, rubbing his hands and sucking a piece of sock, while he rhymed over —"Oh Boys! wont I give it you rightly, tightly, roundly, soundly, Oh Boys! &c."

He seemed to be quite delighted at the idea of the exercise in which he was about to engage. At scientific experiments, sucking sock, eating figs, and using his thin, ill-fed-looking nippie taws, Steamie was considered a don.

After five o'clock Walter and his class fellows had always two hours clear for play. One of the best places for sport was in the 'cond school, the English class-room. It had a double door, but both doors opened at once, being connected by a bar which left a space of about two feet between. Half a dozen forms and desks, a few light short forms or seats, a teacher's desk on a raised platform—these were nearly all the furnishings in the place. It was a square comfortable room, with every facility for romping, and was a favourite resort on dark evenings when outside amusements could not be carried on. From the ceiling hung three gasaliers of a most inviting kind for any boy who had a mind for trapeze swinging.

One evening a game of "Follow my leader" was in progress, and several good jumps over the forms had been gone through and closely followed up. The trapeze was considered the most difficult item, and generally finished the game. Several lads had already sprung from the form, clutched at the bar, and after swinging backwards and forwards several times, had dropped to the ground. It was now Walter's turn. He made the leap like his leaders, when Skin, who was acting as umpire, (not being game enough to follow) gave his legs a push inwards, just as his fingers touched the bar. Losing even the small hold which he had he came down on his side, arm underneath. For this one of the lads, Joe Gilchrist, gave Skin a thorough drubbing. When Walter rose to his feet he found that his wrist was completely out of joint; but by dint of pulling, his chums managed to bring it right. By this time he had fainted, and when he was brought round, he discovered that he could not move his arm. Gilchrist immediately took him to one of the warders, who sent them up to the sick-room. On arriving they told old Meenie, the nurse, a cock-and-bull story about it.

"O aye," said Meenie, "it'll just be anither mock; y're sic' a lot o' mockin' vepers. Let me see your han'."

An examination of Walter's wrist, which by this time had swollen greatly, soon undeceived her.

"Aye! that's a fine han' ye've gi'en yersel'," she said.

Then with much bustling about, she made Walter put the damaged member into a basin of hot water. While this was going on, Gilchrist was busy teasing Meenie's auld cat, Tam, catching him by the tail and making him yell as loudly as his auld ribs would allow him. In reply to her anxious inquiries, Gilchrist explained to Meenie that Tam was merely coughing. Upon this, he was unceremoniously bundled out by the old dame, and not exactly with blessings either, for he had touched her on a sore point.

Walter kept his hand in the hot water for about half an hour, the while Meenie was getting a bed ready. For Walter, so she had informed him, must sleep in the sick-room that night, and see the doctor next day. This was a great blow for our little friend. He had no idea that he would not get back at once amongst his play-fellows. And yet his arm *did* feel very painful.

He went to bed, but slept very little. Next day the coming of Dr Wood was being closely watched from the windows by three other patients.

All were sitting quietly when the man of medicine came walking in, accompanied by Mammie M'Donald, the matron.

He was rather a tall gentleman, with an unmistakable look of his profession about him. Fixing his eyeglass, he took a few steps into the room, and after surveying his patients, and looking down at Mammie (who always accompanied the doctor to the sick-room), remarked "One more, I see."

"Yes, doctor," she said, "this young lad has had a fall and sprained his arm."

"Let me see your arm my boy," said the doctor in a kindly manner.

Walter held out the injured limb to the best of his ability, and anxiously awaited the verdict.

"H'm," ejaculated Dr Wood, "very serious sprain, very serious. What are you applying to it, nurse?"

"Bran bags and hot leeniment, Sir," said Meenie.

"Just continue the same treatment, nurse," said the doctor; and turning round to Walter he said, "Give the arm as much rest as you possibly can and perhaps you will be able to be downstairs in two or three weeks."

Hearing this, Walter's heart almost dropped into his shoes. He tried vainly to convince himself that the doctor had said two or three days, but he knew there was no mistake. After he had examined the other cases, Dr Wood left, Mammie and Meenie being supposed to impress his injunctions upon the minds of the young sufferers. The nurses gone and the knaps all left to themselves, the latter compared notes. Two of the cases were allowed out; and so joyful were the convalescents that they danced upon the auld sofa until one would have expected the seat to be quite knocked out of it. Many such dances it had, however, stood in its time.

Walter had his full three weeks of the sick-room. But a very serious case requiring absolute quiet and extreme treatment occurred, which made it necessary to open the west sick-room. This room was on the opposite wing of the hospital and was kept by a nurse very different from old Meenie. Not that Meenie was a bad nurse, but she was a cantankerous old body, always on the "lecture." The one who got her best side was her cat Tam. The old fuffer could do anything but speak, and if it could not speak with its mouth, it spoke very well by signs.

MEENIE AND HER CAT.

One Sunday, Meenie having gone to church, some of the boys conceived the idea of taking revenge on Tam, and accordingly gave him a good hunt with the carpet canes. On the return of his mistress the maltreated animal went to her, and by cries and signs told his tale of woe. Meenie knew in a moment that something had been up in her absence. She taxed the boys with it and punished them for it.

The nurse in the west sick-room was known familiarly as Mary. Mary was a canny creature, and only came when both rooms were in use. She was much respected by the boys and never in any way subjected to annoyance.

CHAPTER III.

After Walter was well and had gone down amongst his chums again he was warmly received. The boys were all very severe on Skin for his cowardly conduct. But Skin could no more change his vicious nature than the leopard can change his spots. It came out at every opportunity. One morning when some of the little ragged boys, who came from a school in the Vennel for the food which had been left over, were carrying out their pitchers, Skin took off their dirty little caps and popped them in amongst the contents. This was too much for some of the knaps. Skin got a proper "muggin'" and was put out of his schools and greens. He had plenty of eyes on him, you may be sure, to see that he kept to the letter of his sentence. Nothing was, in truth, too bad for his mean, selfish nature. He was the sole proprietor of the small panorama which he kept and exhibited for "trash." It was such a bare-faced robbery business that none of the knaps would go to see it. One of the same kind was kept at the top of the 'cond school stairs by a lad named Harvey. It was a good affair in an unpretentious way, and value for your piece of "trash." Skin, on the pretence of seeing it, managed to overturn the small lamp, when the whole thing went up in a blaze.

It got such a battering and thumping by the audience, in an attempt to extinguish the flames, that the entire concern was fairly demolished.

Skin thought of course that now his rival's business was broken up his own would prosper. But he was mistaken; for one or two of the audience, foreseeing the dodge, had

THEATRE ROYAL.

run up to Skin's panorama and demolished it before his arrival.

Now that Walter has had time to get acquainted with the feeding arrangements perhaps a word or two on that point will not be out of place. We may begin with the hall where the boys dined. It was a long room with a recess at each end, one recess having a window and sliding shutters communicating with one of the apartments of the kitchen. Running up the centre were eight tables with forms set at each side. Underneath each table was a cleek for your cap and a shelf for your dose—though you would never put the latter there unless you wished to have it stolen. Round the walls hung some beautifully-framed old portraits of gentlemen of former greatness in connection with the institution. There they were, grimly staring at the boys as they sat at their meals.

Such was the furniture, which seemed no more permanent than the officials — Shinnie, Clyde, Magnus, and Jamie.

Beginning with Monday, there was for breakfast "pot and milk." Any boy who did not relish this could, by staying in after chapel and making the request, have bread and milk instead. Before going further we must, however, analyse the "pot": oatmeal, water, "chucks," with sometimes an odd gas-burner, a cockroach or a beetle The long gas brackets which were pulled to and fro over the huge boilers would account for the burners; and as for the beetles they were accounted for by their own adventurous natures. These accompaniments were generally to be met with in the "chucks," the mealy ones, which would sometimes fill half the plate. The majority of knaps had a decided antipathy to these, though sometimes a curiosity of a boy would be found who devoured them greedily.

At eleven o'clock, while the boys stood round the square, they had "half a dose" doled out by way of lunch.

At one o'clock dinner was served in the hall, grace being said by one of the lawds. Sometimes a little difficulty occurred here. Being suddenly called upon, the lawd would forget whether it was "Gracious God, we have sinned against," &c., or, "Blessed God, in Thee we live and move," &c.; as likely as not, he would give the grace after meat as the grace before. If he did, Shinnie would call out—"Over again, take care now there," amidst a good deal of smothered merriment.

The first course was vegetable broth, always of good quality. Sufficient time having been allowed for its disposal, the wifies carried in on large pewter platters a quantity of meat cut up into small pieces, laying the platters on the ends of the southmost tables.

Presently, they came again with others filled with potatoes. Monitors selected for the purpose, assisted by Jamie and Shinnie, portioned out to each his share; the plates being carried to and fro by waiters also specially appointed. When all had been served, a second share was given to the eldest boys, as far as the remainder would go. A "half dose" was also allowed each boy at dinner time.

At five o'clock came bread and milk, and at eight "pot" and milk, some boys, as in the morning, having bread and milk instead.

On Tuesday the meals were the same, except that for dinner there was Irish stew with, of course, potatoes and bread. Wednesday brought rice soup, potatoes, and bread; Thursday, potato soup of a very superior quality (the big cook had great credit for her "tout soup"), roast beef, and bread. Friday, there were "pea claw," "cone," "touts" and "chit," with sometimes broth or rice soup by way of a change.

On Saturday any boy could have dinner if he chose to order it. On Sunday there were "chit," "butt," eggs, and milk, and occasionally rice and milk or "plum pud."

On the whole, a boy with the most particular taste could not say that he was not well fed, and that, too, in a most cleanly manner. Nevertheless, there were some who felt dissatisfied with the regulation fare and pilfered the carrots and turnips out of the kitchen. Skin and some of his scogies were always on the "nab," quietly creeping in by the kitchen door. The little lobby was usually well covered with sand and they had to proceed with the utmost caution if they did not want to "catch a tartar" in the shape of the wee cook.

Among Walter's friends there were some good story-tellers who helped to wile away many an hour on the long evenings after tea.

A little fellow, Neillie Angus, had a rare gift in that way. Two or three of the kids after a little coaxing would get him to come into their parlour, and taking their seats round a roaring fire the company would be kept in great amusement by Neillie's diverting little tales.

One evening, Angus having gone away tired, one of Walter's friends whispered to him that he had a good trick "if he wisna fud."

"All right," replied Walter, "what is it?"

"Here," said Turner, handing Walter a piece of shoe-lace, "you do what I do."

After whispering some instructions, at which Walter chuckled a good deal, Turner touched his piece of lace or "pint" at the gas and motioned to Walter to do the same.

Looking stealthily into the lawds' parlour they saw some of their majesties seated at the long tables. One had the

Illustrated London News and was deeply interested, no doubt, in some of the military manœuvres of the Austrian War; another was pegging away at a continued story in *All the Year Round;* a third was sketching some of the illustrated capital letters from *Punch;* two or three were having a quiet game at honours; and several others were engaged in various peaceful amusements.

Walter and his friend, taking a table each, slipped quietly underneath, carrying with them their piece of boot lace burning like a fuse. The first boy Walter came to was he of the *Illustrated London News*, who was probably criticising the stupidity of the Danes in allowing the Austrians to lay their mines so near as to blow up their outworks. Walter underneath, looking at his outstretched legs and feet, quietly touched his boot laces in several places with his piece of smouldering "pint." Everywhere that he touched a little red spark was left which slowly and surely wandered all over the lace. The same was done to each of the lawds, and then Walter and Turner stole from their cover unobserved.

An obtrusive smell arising caused one of the youths to look underneath the table. There he saw what appeared to him to be a host of glow-worms moving about. Every lawd's boot was without its fixings; and it would have gone hard with the conspirators had they been caught.

Shortly after this, a sad occurrence happened. A little fellow named Macglashan took suddenly ill and died. The gloom cast over all by the event could hardly be credited. All play and romps were hushed entirely and every one conversed in whispers. At the ordinary day-school a death may cause no more than a simple remark, but in the

"Wark," where in a manner a kind of brotherhood existed, each one felt it very keenly.

However, after the funeral was past and matters had got into their old cheery rut, an event of quite a different kind was about to take place. Some of the lawds and cholds were to give a representation of a piece entitled "The Life and Death of Dick Turpin." They had been at practice for some time during spare hours. Swords, daggers, and pistols had been made in the turning-house, and the preparations were complete.

On the Friday when the stirring spectacle was to take place the evening meal was hastily disposed of, and a rush made for "Cockie's," which was the class-room fixed upon. The desks were placed round the room and on the top of them the forms were piled, making a very respectable gallery indeed. When all were seated some of the warders came in, giving a tone of extra distinction and respectability to the audience from their being accommodated with the Royal Box, otherwise Cockie's desk.

The first cornet of the Wark's band had been pressed into service in lieu of an orchestra. He was seated on the right side of the gallows, which, by the way, was the blackboard frame.

The lights having been lowered, and everything got into set for a highway scene, the cornet struck up a bar or two, the wee room door opened, and in came Cockie Smith *alias* Dick Turpin.

Cockie softly threaded his way and felt about him, one fancied, further than his hands could go (using that stage walk peculiar to bold bad characters of a murderous type when the stage is in semi-darkness). Stopping short, Dick exclaims "Ha ha," then walks another step and swaying himself backwards and forwards proceeds: "Ha, ha! this waning light but serves to make the darkness visible. What! A footstep! Who comes? Yes! No! Yes, 'tis he! Ha, ha! I shall lie in wait under this precipice's shade."

He throws himself down in front of the school-room coal-box which represents a rock.

THE "ACTING."

The cornet plays up slow music; the gas is slightly turned up (unfortunately the gas pendants were in the centre of the room and a boy had to take a chair to do this); the door again opens and another character enters as deliberately as the first.

"Foiled again," says Character No. 2. "He could not have passed this way or I should have seen his tracks on this springy turf. Ho, ho! ho, ho! Ha, ha! I have sworn to track him to the ends of the earth."

Dick, springing up, utters the one word "Villain!" Then the other villain, after a pause and a long look, exclaims—"What! Dick, my long lost friend!"

"What! is this really you, Tom?"

By this time the gas had been turned full on and Dick and Tom stood hand in hand, the cornet at this moment striking in with "Hielandman! Hielandman! come to your tatties," a tune which Walter thought singularly inappropriate.

It was really a sight. The two villains were dressed nearly alike—jacket and vest off, stockings drawn up over foot of trousers, an old belt round the waist stuck full of wooden daggers, creases, and pistols. Having forgotten their lines, and all their ha, ha's and ho, ho's having been fully expended, it was a perfect tableau. After mutual explanations they agreed to work together for their joint revenge—"Ha, ha!"

They perpetrated fearful robberies upon some peaceful knaps who, with their coats turned outside in and with other slight transformations, walked out and in for the special benefit of that murderous couple who plied their unlawful business to an alarming extent. This finished the first Act or the *life*.

After a solo from the cornet ("O where, tell me where"), the bell was rung on the back of the wee room door with a piece of a slate frame. Out came Dick on horseback. Rushing round the arena (of course Black Bess upon whose shoulders Dick sat was one of the other boys) he kept shouting "They follow, they follow."

Almost immediately, in rode another, boot and saddle, the same way. This was Dick's friend, Tom King. After they had trotted about the room for a time, a great noise was heard in the wee room, and again the cry "They follow, they follow." With this there arrived about twenty fierce-looking policemen with their jackets inside out and wearing great black soot moustaches, every man mounted on a horse. This was considered the spectacular part, where all the odd people and supers had an opportunity to shine. Here commenced the grand chase.

Each of the audience picking out a favourite encouraged him — sometimes man, sometimes horse. They galloped round to the infinite delight of the knaps.

At last the gallant Tom was caught, tried, and sentenced to be hanged by the neck till dead. The black board at this juncture became very useful, being really not unlike a gallows.

Poor Tom King was swung off amid great applause. At the death of Black Bess sympathy ran high, not so much for Bess as for Cockie Smith who got a severe fall; for it so happened that just at the time when Bess drops dead, a little imp of a kid having got under the desks put out his leg, over which Bess fell just about two seconds sooner and I daresay about five seconds quicker than it was proposed between her and Dick. However, the last kick was got over very creditably and Bess was carried into the side room, the cornet blaring out "See the conquering hero comes," which was the stock tune with the "Wark's band."

After a wait of about ten minutes the scene was changed. Now they were to have what was termed the "clown stuff." The prompter rang the bell; in tumbled clown and pantaloon.

Their get-up was rather good, and what between stealing clothes and parcels (the contents of which they fairly divided between them) from passers-by, and then literally smashing the policemen, a very effective wind-up was given to the affair.

The only objectionable thing was the treatment of the supers. If the clown had to kick a man he did it most effectually: if he had to hit him over the head with a slate he made no mere pretence at the business. Nothing in short was missed that would add to the effect, and in the melee at the finish there were not a few hard knocks.

CHAPTER IV.

ONE day Walter and some of his comrades were surprised to see a large number of mallets, chisels, &c., generally used by stone-cutters, lying beside one of the pillars. Much speculation as to what was about to be done followed the discovery. Everyone had a different idea.

"Here's a fine chance ony way for a bit o' fun," suggested Gilchrist. "We'll plank them." No sooner said than done. Willing hands got the tools together, and taking them to a trap leading into a drain just in front of the kitchen connie down went the lot. The trap was a large, square, box-shaped drain into which the huge tubfuls of slops were emptied.

Just at this juncture some talking was heard at the pend gate, and the delinquents disappeared instantly. A gentleman and two masons came into the quadrangle. After some conversation, a ball of twine was produced, certain measurements were taken, and by chalking the cord a set of lines had soon been got round the square. On the workmen looking for their tools, of course they could nowhere be found.

They inquired at the lodge, and search was made in every conceivable corner. The hunt was still going on when

Fummie and another of the servants came out with a large tubful of water in which the "pot" plates, &c., had been washed.

Up went the lid of the trap, and down went the contents of the tub on the top of the workmen's tools. Such a mess! And such a row! In fact, the workmen remarked that if they had dreamt of this kind of thing happening they would have had nothing whatever to do with the job.

Gilchrist and Walter were amongst the greatest sympathisers, promising the masons that in future they would keep a strict watch on their tools, and see that no one touched them. For this much the men thanked them, at the same time cursing the imps who had played them such a trick.

Going up to the sixth school, where some of the boys were larking, one of the masters came in to put away his books into a cupboard where they were kept. This was the French teacher, Mr Chaumont. One of the bigger boys suggested to Crighton that he should go up to old Frenchie and say, "Parley-vou Frongsay, Mongsu." The old man (such was the representation) liked so much to hear the young boys speak to him in his own language. Up went Walter, and looking into the dominie's face (he was one of the methodical old gentlemen) asked him if he could speak in his own mother tongue! Walter's answer was a bang on the ear, accompanied with the remark, "It's thee same song ev-er-ee day, thee same song ev-er-ee day." It was only another little item in Walter's education. He was certainly not likely ever to forget that particular phrase from the flowery language of France.

Next day was Halloween, and the boys were to have a treat—" yaps and nits." They all formed round the quadrangle and the wardsmen presently arrived carrying large baskets filled with apples, some of the elder boys following with basketfuls of nuts. These were distributed in handfuls, to receive which each boy held out his cap. After all had got their shares, they broke up, some to pay debts—" what

THE "WARK" BAND.

they were awn "—some to sell, others to " skech " or " cadge," and a few to enjoy what they had received. Some of the younger knaps and kids had hardly anything for themselves, their share having gone to make up a dollop for some of the older boys. For example, Skin was laden with nine and a half apples, and every one of his pockets was filled with nuts; while others of the same fraternity were even more heavily burdened. These stolen portions they would perhaps sell over again to the poor little duffers from whom they had been "skeched," or perhaps they were eaten in a miserly manner, "chawing" their neighbours.

Occasionally in the mornings the "Wark's band" would favour the boys with a selection from—well, no matter what, they always managed to provide something noisy between brass, skin, and a pair of big full-toned cymbals. There was Taylor, the big drummer. After he gave three formal raps on the hide, all the other instruments came into action, and the sound in the square was as if a bombardment were going on. The word "double" would be given, and the band, striking up "Old Grannie Cockalee," what with right wheel and left wheel, there was soon a regular Pharaoh's serpent of boys, acquiring a good appetite for their "pot," especially on a cold winter morning.

Walter was quite at home now. He had made a few friends as well as a number of enemies. There were Ross, Gilchrist, Smith, and Walter M'Lennan, all capital fellows. M'Lennan was as fleet as the wind, he was the fastest without doubt in his own set, and was generally the first choice in any game where speed was necessary.

The nights were drawing in. It was almost dark by six o'clock, and all games had to be carried on inside the pend gate unless some amusement was got on the pretence of going to the well in the 'ird greens. Then the boys would take a scurry in the dark; or perhaps there would be a scare from some threatened invasion of keelies from Heriot Bridge and the Grassmarket. In that case a sally would be made across the greens towards the shrubbery to meet the imaginary foe. Many deeds of great prowess were done in the dark.

In reality, there was no damage done unless to a brick wall which divided the auld wifie's garden from the shrubbery, or perhaps to a window or two in the locality. The storming party would then return, their hearts swelling with victory, and no doubt glad to be relieved from the outside darkness.

Retiring to the kids' parlour, Walter and some others strung up their doses before the fire, and soon had a jolly steaming "fan toast." A pack of cards was produced and a game at honours, supplemented by a few stories, put past the evening until time for the "learning."

It was nearing the Christmas holidays, and a great deal of talk now went on as to what they were going to do, where they were going to spend the time, and so on. One interesting occupation was the making of the paper bags to hold the cake and bun which each boy received when he left for home. A number of copy books were secured and the leaves sewn into large square bags into which the good things were to be put when breaking-up-day came; that time being carefully calculated, not only by days, but by hours and minutes.

On the afternoon before Christmas Day they followed in line into the store, where each received a small, round, seed cake covered on the top with red sugar and having the letters G. H. H. in white, as well as a square cake of shortbread and two oranges.

On the large deal table was a pile of "doses," for which no one had any concern at present, whether they were "auld or new baken, fan or plain." It seemed as if the big-handled knife with which Shinnie cut the "doses" in two was going to have its holidays as well. The large bin for the meal, and the beer barrel on its stout gauntrees were quietly ignored, although, at any other time the contents of the latter would very probably have been tested if the chances had been in favour of the knaps.

Old Clyde, Shinnie's dog, sat blinking at each boy as he received his lot, as much as to say, "Take care of bun fever, my boy." When the recipients arrived outside, the bun and cake were bagged in the paper pock, and were rolled up in the black bag which contained their change of clothing, &c.

Walter and his chums made their way out, clear of the "Wark" until the second day of January.

On the return of the boys to the hospital they all seemed to have enjoyed themselves thoroughly. There was no case of illness other than what Meenie could soon put right without the doctor's advice or aid.

Many stories of adventure and sight-seeing were recounted for the benefit of those who had been in the "Wark" during the holiday. One little fellow, who with great energy tried to describe what he saw in the pantomime, was christened and known ever afterwards in the "Wark" as "The Clown."

The snow was still on the ground to the depth of nearly two feet, having fallen very heavily during the holidays. Now was the time to punish the detestable "tellers," who had made their companions suffer in many instances for very slight offences, their only desire being to get into favour with the wardsmen or other officials, who often received information from them quite unasked. There are few school-boys who do not hate the very name of "tell-tale," and who do not entertain a most thorough dislike for those who bear it. But in Heriot's Hospital the tell-tale was looked upon rather in the light of a criminal, who was not only detected but was punished at every opportunity.

George Heriot's Hospital.   51

For the first day or two after the holidays the educational department was not quite so rigorously carried on as usual; and as the boys were encouraged rather than otherwise in larking amongst the snow full freedom was given to them in the greens. In fact they were allowed to do pretty much as they pleased, within rational bounds. Sides were chosen and snowballing was indulged in until all were tired out.

A SNOW HOUSE.

Then they set to to make huge snowballs, with which a snowhouse was built, leaving a small doorway to be closed up with other material at hand. A search was made for two or three of the tellers who had distinguished themselves during the "half." When they had been captured they were pushed into the snow-house, crying and struggling, and the door blocked up. It was no jerry-built fabric either, but a strong and solid prison, and by the time the unfortunates

managed to see daylight again, they were both tired and
sore. No doubt they would think twice before incurring
the risk of having themselves put into the same place again.

Next day the snow-house was re-built in the model of a
fort, and the battle of the "seventh greens" was fought,
with the lawds in the fort and the cholds and knaps as the
attacking party; the fight was both fierce and long, and it
was hard to say who had gained the victory. At last a cheer
rang out, in unison with the Wark dinner bell calling the
knaps to their "tout-soup," to which they did ample justice
that day.

When they reached the square they found Dr Bedford
standing in conversation with some one at Mammie's "connie."
One of the knaps conceived the notion of trying to see how
the Doctor would take a "taste of the weather." Accordingly
he let fly a snowball which whizzed past the Doctor's head
and flattened itself on the chapel wall. The Doctor took no
notice, which gave encouragement to another little chap
who tried a second shot. This time the aim was more
precise, as the Doctor's soft-felt "wide-awake" testified.
Turning round with a smile on his face, Dr Bedford was
about to remark that he was satisfied, or something to that
effect, when two or three more let fly at once. Seeing
that the time was not one for parley (and it was not in the
Doctor to be ill-natured), he gathered his cloak about his
ears and made over the square to his own quarters. On
reaching the Govies' door, he turned to the boys and
rewarded them with a playful shake of the head; after
which he immediately disappeared. It was well for him
that he did, for the door which he had just shut showed
in a moment what he would have got. This evidence of

good feeling on the part of Dr Bedford told with marked effect upon the boys, who were jubilant over their little bit of fun.

The lawds' examination had come and gone and a new set of boys were in their places. This raised Walter and his friends a step higher, entitling them to the rank of knaps. Among the new boys were two little fellows from London, who made great sport for the rest. They

LEVICK'S WARD.

were asked by the knaps, from the youngest to the oldest, to repeat Scottish guttural words, and in attempting to do so they of course utterly failed.

Walter had a shift from the eighth to the seventh ward, a long room containing about thirty beds, situated on the east side of the quadrangle. Levick, the gate-keeper, had charge of this ward, which accordingly took its name from him. At one end of the room there was an enclosure for the nurse of the eighth ward.

The first night happened to be bath night, when each one having divested himself of all but shirt and trousers, and carrying his towel, they marched off single-file downstairs and through the dark seventh school and museum into the "'cond" school. In the floor was a large, open trap-door from which a bright light was streaming, and through which came sounds of the splashing of bathers below. Here the boys had to halt, and, like a host of phantoms, wait their turn. Some had their towels tied fantastically round their

THE BATH.

heads; others were switching their neighbours with a wetted end of the towel.

After a wait of about three or four minutes, the boys of the fifth and sixth wards came popping up through the trap, and amidst some passing chaff Levick's lads disappeared into the regions of steam.

At the bottom of the stair or ladder there was a long stone cistern about two feet wide and deep, used for washing the feet; and on the left were two large zinc baths. The wall space was filled up with pegs for hanging clothes on; and there were three hand-basins for the use of the warders during the daytime, &c.

The boys went into the bath, and after a lavish application of soap, the orders were given—"Over the head," "over the head," "over the head," "out." Passing through the shower bath (and a cold one it was), a brisk rubbing with the coarse towel soon brought a healthy glow to each and all. Their scanty clothing donned, a smart double trot brought the boys to their ward. Kneeling at their little stools they said prayers, Levick giving two knocks on the table with a cloth brush to indicate that enough time had been allowed for devotions. Then every one jumped into bed in good condition for a sound night's rest.

CHAPTER V.

WALTER was getting on well with his education, and his report was "very satisfactory." It was nearing the time when the lawds and cholds would have to be preparing their scudding balls for June day. A month was required to make a number of those articles, very necessary for assisting in the celebration of George Heriot's birthday.

If the Herioter is famed for mischief, he should also be famed for ball-making. The care bestowed, the exactness observed in the smallest particulars as to form and weight, and the gauging when being finished in the rolling, really required an apprenticeship.

For the making of a ball the necessary requisites were: cork, willies, worsted, leather (or sheepskin), strong white linen thread, and a good needle. The cork was cut into a little round ball, and great pains bestowed on the foundation. No matter how well the ball might be finished outside, if care were not taken at the start, and carried all through the making, it was sure to turn out a "dift" or a "buckin' stoter." Sometimes a short quill was inserted into the cork; and a few small shot or sparrow hail put into the quill made what was called a rattler. The willies were wound round the cork carefully and firmly until a diameter of about an inch-and-a-quarter had been obtained. The worsted was then rolled round in a damp state, one or two turns at a time. Every six turns or so a pressure on a wall or some solid substance was good for the ball. It

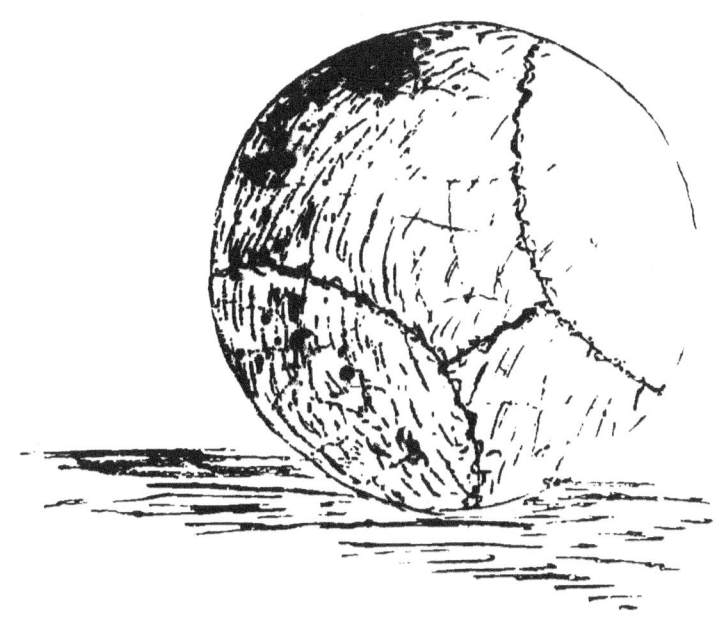

A HERIOT BALL—EXACT SIZE.

gave the chance to tighten the worsted. Proceeding, care had to be exercised in keeping the ball perfectly round until it had attained a size of about two-and-three-sixteenth inches. The skin had then to be prepared by cutting for the ball three pieces, a middle bit and two tops. These had to be thoroughly wetted, rubbed between the fingers and stretched, by which preparation they became very thin. The first to be fixed on was the middle piece. This was sewn in front by about half-an-inch of the leather; the extra part was then cut and trimmed with a pair of scissors; after which the top of one end was sewn on. Turning the ball, the same was done with the other end.

As to the stitch (which was particularly neat in a well-made ball), that is not so easily explained. It requires to be seen to be understood, and anyone who desires to see it may examine the very choice collection of prize balls in the Edinburgh Museum of Science and Art.

Some of the lawds and cholds were beginning to get together the necessary articles. The tailors in the vicinity were being "cadged for willies," while Mammie and the wifies were courted for old stockings. Cuttings of sheep-skin, often whole skins, were purchased and systematically marked off into separate parts with very little waste. It was a profitable business, for a good ball could easily command a "sye" or sixpence on June Day. The old socks were sometimes distributed among the boys so that all had a chance.

So far the work of ball-making went on briskly. The kids and younger knaps were pressed into the service of the elder boys.

Some were running the worsted into little bunches; others were busy in the corner of the 'ird greens at the well, a six-sided pillar with four moveable pipes and rusty tinnies (when there were any), rubbing and scrubbing at the bits of leather till their little fingers were purple. Nevertheless, it had to be well washed and stretched.

otherwise there would be a "muggin'," and they would be sent to do it over again.

Some of the younger makers put proper "ghosts" out of their hands—"difts," as they were called. A good "dift" would generally rebound about six inches from the ground.

A "buckin' stoter," perhaps a well though carelessly made ball, would stot six feet, if your eye or your neighbour's nose did not get in its way. But a well-made ball would rise to the 'ist millar, easily, and endanger no one. Often the makers would use up odds and ends of material for making what were called "nackets" or small balls. They were very neat, although useless things for scudding.

The boys had begun to practise the vocal part of their programme, Heriot's birthday song, the anthem, &c., for June Day. Mr Hunter, the singing master, was busy drilling the knaps — no light task seeing that no knap had any taste for contralto, tenor, or alto; every one must be "a bawser," and it was not easy for our teacher to rattle the little old-fashioned box of dominoes or harmonium (which was wisely kept locked up in a press in the sixth school) to a choir of some forty bass voices. Still, some of them did condescend to become "July squeekers" for the time being.

MR HUNTER.

Laubach was also vainly endeavouring to point out to the members of the "Wark band" that at certain parts "you must ta-ta, ta-ta-ta very softilee, and not so kvick." But alas for his instructions! The cymbals, triangle, and drum thought they had as much right to bring their instruments into prominence as the first cornet, and June Day was too good an opportunity to be lost.

It was now the Friday before the great event; and in the evening the knaps and several of the out-door school children were taken to Greyfriars Church for a preliminary rehearsal. The Heriot and George Watson boys, the Merchant Maidens, and the Trades Maidens were shown their different positions in the body of the church. After rehearsal they marched to the greens, where Muscle Doo and his men had been very busy for the last two or three days fixing up posts and dividing the space into sections with cords, little boards being fixed up with the names of the various Heriot schools. Here, also, there was a short rehearsal, followed usually by a smart shower of rain, which was taken as a good omen, although it dispersed the gathering rather abruptly.

The Saturday passed somewhat wearily with the knaps. On their coming into the Wark in the evening, all were delighted to see that the buskin' had commenced. The two pillars at each side of "Geordie" had been covered with rhododendron leaves. The rhododendron bush, the knaps held as "Geordie's." The sock business was rather brisk, and the sale of a few balls had been effected, several of the knaps having been commissioned to secure one or more good specimens for auld callant friends. Sunday was put in quietly, the knaps lying about the greens in groups, talking of the morrow, or stringing together long chains of daisies, which were called "knaps" after themselves. The dandelion flowers were called "neets"; buttercups were Merchant Maidens; and the emblem of the Trades Maidens, which always was the Heriotties' favourite, was the clover flower.

Bed-time brought little sleep for the knaps, who were eager for the morning. Walter, Gilchrist, Toby, Sinclair, McGregor, and a number of the lads in the seventh ward had, in fact, made it up not to sleep that night. They would "keep waken"—so they declared—to watch for the streak of daylight when the buskin' would begin. Several stories went round, but one by one the boys dropped off to sleep, until at length all had succumbed.

The sun was high, and as bright a morning as ever smiled upon June Day greeted Gilchrist when he awoke. He was the first in the ward to spring to his feet, and in making for the window he gave Walter a shake. The sight of such a morning brought loud exclamations of admiration, which roused a number of the others. There it was, the first sight of June Day morning in all its glory.

The whole side of the square, above the pend gate, was transformed as if by magic into a perfect fairy scene with flowers and leaves. The statue of George Heriot stood in a bower of green leaves and blossoms. On either side two huge letters—G. H.—made up with lilies filled the blank between the statue and the schoolroom windows. In front was a large shield with horn-shaped trophies, decorated with flowers of all kinds and colours, the crown being a mass of roses and fruit.

Above that again was a smaller horn of plenty, on the top of which some of the most tempting apples and oranges

THE RUSKINS.

were fixed. Underneath was a long band of metal, ribbon-shaped, on which were painted in gold letters the words, "I distribute cheerfully." Under that was a long heavy festoon of leaves and twigs reaching from end to end of the wall. To the trellis of the museum windows were attached shields and devices carefully and artistically wrought out in beautiful blossom, and bearing on them the goldsmiths' hammer.

The same kind of thing was carried up to the "barty," on the top of which was a huge crimson crown, rich with velvet and roses, and with small flags and bannerettes affixed. Large flags were flaunting from the "'cond" school, the writing school, the seventh school, and the fifth ward windows. These made up the decorations of the square on the north side.

Peter the gardener, and one or two of the lawds, were giving the finishing touch to the whole by putting a choice bouquet into the hand of George Heriot's statue.

A shout of delight resounded through the Wark as this was accomplished, all the ward windows being crowded with boys watching the proceedings. Then all was noisy with laughter and merriment. Every boy was awake and up, except Toby.

"Oh, the sleepy nugget," said Sinclair; "let us gie him a muggin'."

"A dookin'," shouted another.

A "coup" was, however, agreed upon, and two or three of the boys got up to Toby's bedside. Before many seconds he was kissing the floor, with the bedding and the mattress above him. Crawling out from underneath and rubbing his head in a rueful manner, he looked from one bed to another and saw that each contained a snoring sleeper. He could not make it out. However, the smothered laughter soon revealed to him that he was a victim. Being a good-natured fellow he passed over the incident with a laugh, and all was soon noise and fun again.

It was not often that the boys lay in eager anticipation of the ringing of the "rising" bell, but this morning, as its welcome sound pealed through the square, everyone was stirring; some, in fact, were nearly ready before the bell had ceased to toll. Running down the square, a general inspection was made of all the decorations, and numerous comments were made by some of the older boys as to wherein the present differed from former buskings. The general verdict was that it looked much the same as they had always seen it look.

The "connies" were taken up by some of the lawds to practise scudding, for the purpose of keeping their hand in. Others were trying for "skinned ba's doufed." They had a ball with a long string attached, which was thrown up until it rested beside another ball lying in the rhone; then with a sharp twitch they perhaps chanced to bring down the doufed ball, which, if a well-made one, was as good as fourpence at least to the lucky thrower.

Chapel time coming round, all were marched into prayers. After breakfast, the order was to dress. To-day, every article of the knaps' attire was new from cap to boots. But what did it matter? tight buttons or corn squeezers, all were happy.

By about half-past ten each one was dressed and ready. The boys of the band were especially neat in their vests of spotless white dimity, ornamented with blue enamel buttons and a gold-coloured band about an inch and a half deep round their caps.

A goodly number of visitors were beginning to arrive and were having a general look about; and the knaps now realised that June-Day had really come. When the bell rang, all were arranged in order to proceed to church. Marching out they went on their way rejoicing, which was rather unusual on the way to church. Arriving at Greyfriars, they took their seats, as had been arranged on the Friday before, and presently had the pleasure of seeing the Govies, headed by the Lord Provost, filing into the gallery.

The preliminary services over, a sermon was preached from the 14th verse of the 90th Psalm—"Satisfy us early with Thy mercy." Then there was an anthem, "The earth is the Lord's and the fulness thereof," very creditably performed. After which a prayer and a chant brought the service to an end.

As they emerged from the gate in the Wark's wall on the way back a full view was obtained of the "'ird" greens. And what a sight it was! The ground was completely covered with school children and their friends. Going up by the stairs leading to the terrace the boys were marched alongside the balusters and downstairs into their position in front of the platform.

By this time everything was pretty well in order and waiting for the celebration proper to begin. A hushed silence was over all and everybody was evidently impatient for the officials to appear.

On the balustrade over a thousand spectators had taken up their positions; the green with its rows of out-door school children and teachers was closely packed, old scholars—

little sisters and big sisters, little brothers and big brothers —and the parents of little ones being gathered at the back all along the banks. The happy smiling faces, the gay attire of all present, and the bright warm sunshine made a delightful picture : and the general effect upon the mind of the thoughtful onlooker was a feeling of gratitude to the generous founder of such a noble institution.

After a wait of a few minutes, the silence was broken by a tremendous noise proceeding from the square, growing gradually louder, forming itself into the air, "Cheer, Boys, Cheer," as the band emerged from under the pend gate and marched to the front of the steps, where they finished their performance in fine style. Descending the stairs the players took up their position immediately in front of the knaps, in a little semicircle.

By this time the Lord Provost, Magistrates, and Governors had taken their stand on the steps, dressed in their gay robes of office. Mr Hunter on going to the platform announced that they would sing that spirited song "The Merry Month of June."

> Then would the thousand voices raise
> And sing the themes to Geordie's praise,
> We'll ne'er forget it a' our days
> Where'er we be,
> And keep the merry day in June,
> Though ower the sea.

The verses went well, and were sung in a hearty manner, many of the auld callants joining in. The song is as under.

THE MERRY MONTH OF JUNE.

> The merry month of June,
> Of sunny days and flow'rs,
> Sets ev'ry heart in tune,
> And leads the lightsome hours :

Glad Nature's voice bids all rejoice,
But we have bliss apart from this,
We hail the day with grateful mirth
Which brings to mind George Heriot's birth,
    Which brings to mind George Heriot's birth.

    Tho' centuries have 'lapsed,
    Since Heriot lived and died,
    His bounty, like a stream,
    Still flows, a golden tide,
And hearts bereav'd, by him reliev'd,
From year to year, shall gather here,
And hail the day with grateful mirth
Which brings to mind George Heriot's birth,
    Which brings to mind George Heriot's birth.

    No hero's praise we sing,
    Far worthier is our theme :
    'Twas love for fellow-man
    That prompted Heriot's scheme,
Our father he, his children we,
It fits us well his worth to tell,
And hail the day with grateful mirth
Which brings to mind George Heriot's birth,
    Which brings to mind George Heriot's birth.

The Lord Provost then took his stand on the platform, speaking to the children in a pleasant manner, telling them in a few brief sentences of the large-heartedness of George Heriot, and how they should show their appreciation of his having so bountifully provided for them. He also exhorted those who had already partaken of the benefits of the institution to persevere in making the best use of the knowledge they had gained, and the precepts they had been taught. He complimented Dr Bedford on the robust, healthy, and happy appearance of his boys, and took the opportunity of thanking his colleagues on the Governing Body for their unwearied endeavours in promoting everything so as to gain the most satisfactory results. In closing, he expressed the wish that everyone might enjoy a happy afternoon.

Mr Hunter then intimated another song—

WHILE GRATITUDE FILLS EVERY BREAST.

While gratitude fills every breast, and happy faces shine,
While memory twines her laurel wreath round Heriot's
    hallow'd shrine.
        Come swell the gladdening strain
        Again, and yet again !
Awake the cheerful song of praise, let youthful rapture reign !
For loving was his noble heart, and bountiful his hand,
Whose honour'd name shall long adorn the annals of our land.

'Mid honest Labour's humble homes, his Temples, wide-
    renown'd,
Like oaks amid the forest grove, tower gracefully around ;
        While Learning's golden smile
        Beams o'er the cultur'd soil.
To foster, with her gentle light, the lowly flowers of toil !
O sweetly may they blossom fair in Virtue's kindly shade,
And may the star of Wisdom shine, ere all their beauties fade !

Now while our Founder's cherished worth each youthful breast
    inspires,
March on, with steady step and true, like sons of hardy sires !
        A cheer !—a joyful cheer,
        For Heriot's name so dear !
O fondly, in our grateful hearts, that name we will revere !
For while old Scotia rears her crest, majestic and serene,
His fame, immortal as her own, shall flourish ever green !

This performance over, Dr Bedford proposed a vote of thanks to the Lord Provost for presiding on the occasion and for the few well-directed remarks made to his boys, which, he had no doubt would be remembered and taken to heart, so that when they came to be auld callants, the Provost might still have reason to retain his high opinion of them as citizens of Edinburgh. In his (the Doctor's) knowledge many of the auld callants had risen to positions of eminence, both civic and professional. He remarked that unfortunately the few badly-behaved young men who left the Hospital were generally well known, while the hundreds of well-behaved boys were seldom heard of. At the same time he would say from his own knowledge that, if the names of the prosperous and successful auld callants were before the people of Edinburgh (which he hoped before long it would be in his power to put) they would be greatly surprised, and their opinion of the old Herioters entirely changed.

Dr Bedford was heartily cheered, and the band struck up "God save the Queen," in which all joined heartily. As this was considered the end of the ceremony, the school children were marched back to their different schools, where each one received a large bun and orange. The knaps filed into the hall, where a capital pie was provided, after which there were oranges and figs, instead of the glass of wine formerly given.

The Govies and some of the parents of the boys had also gone into the hall. Here another short speech was delivered by the Provost, who with George Heriot's loving cup in his hand, pledged the memory of the founder in a few appropriate remarks, the cup afterwards being handed round among the Governors and a few of their friends.

Grace after meat having been said by one of the lawds, all adjourned to the square. Here was another sight which gladdened the heart of the knap. The auld caliants were scudding. It was a time for the youngsters to look and learn, and for the elder boys to sell their balls.

The square at this time was no place for old people or children, for what consideration has an auld callant for frailty of age, when heated up by scudding in some of the "connies"?

When the ball takes a spin across the square, he makes a dash after it, with his heart beating at the thought of old times, bringing to mind the many thousand chases he has had in the same place as a boy.

He cannot brook interference upon any account. Looking over to Mammie's "connie," one sees a set of about a dozen callants stotting and striking the ball in a manner entirely peculiar to the old Heriottie.

Up it goes against the wall, just a little above the first millar, and with such a force that it rebounds nearly to the centre of the square. That was a good stroke. It is now caught up again by Walter Clerk, who, with another send, makes it again birl outwards. Then the cry of "keep it up" is heard, and the ball is deftly caught by McNaughton, who, without gripping it, turns its course to the ground, and with some tact sends it under his left arm, round his back, again towards the wall. This time, however, it strikes against the tirlies and falls to the ground.

The ball comes into play again, but the scudder is a bad one. Thinking that height is a good point he sends the ball into the rhone. A murmur of disapprobation runs round the players at this display of ignorance. However, another knap manages to sell another ball. "Doufing" was the life of trade in that business.

A number of sight-seers, while looking at the decorations, got rather severely knocked about, and complained vehemently that such a dangerous game should be allowed to go on. Foolish people. Did they not know that the square was made expressly for scudding? That, at least, is the auld callant's opinion.

Passing out through the pend gate, our friends Crighton, Sutherland, Ross, and a few others made their way down to the greens. Here great fun was in progress. Jing-go-rings were well patronised by the youngsters; and such a a kissing and a smacking! The knaps were well taken out by the "judies," especially the band boys. Passing from this green to the other brought our young friends to the Greyfriars gate, emerging from which they took a turn round by Forrest Road and back into the grounds by the front entrance.

Walking up the terrace, in front of them were half-a-dozen boys much older than any of our friends, and belonging to George Watson's Hospital on the opposite side of Lauriston. As they passed, one of the "neets" made a remark which raised the ire of Gilchrist, who gave some cheek in return. This led to one of the strangers using his fists rather freely, but a stoppage was put to the fray before it came to anything serious. It was but a temporary stoppage however. As the spark had been lit there was sure to be a fire. The knaps passed into the Wark smarting with indignation at being attacked in their own castle, and at a time of peace too. Going into the square, they complained to some of the lawds, who at once called a council of war. The decision was immediate expulsion; and so, round the greens went the band of lawds, who cleared out all the "neets" by the run.

By this time the clock was proclaiming the hour of four. That put a sudden stop to the dancing, the jing-go rings and the other games that were then in progress. The warders went round, and the place was soon cleared. A second gathering was formed in the West Meadows, and the games were continued until a late hour.

That night on Walter reaching the square a good number of the knaps had arrived. They were making sad havoc among the oranges on the horn of plenty at Geordie's feet, trying for them with difts and old balls.

Groups of boys were scattered about talking over the day's events, the most interesting item for discussion being the attack on the kids by the neets. Some were for immediate satisfaction; others advised mature consideration and delay.

CHAPTER VI.

THE following day was a holiday, which gave an opportunity for the taking down of the decorations. Walter, Gilchrist, Ross, and a few others had agreed to meet, and an outing was taken at Royston.

The tide was out when they arrived and a mussel-hunting expedition was proposed. Away they went, and jumping over the stones were soon well laden. Coming back, Tait slipped and went head first into a large pool of water. It was an unfortunate little accident, but Tait soon got over it by spreading his clothes out on the sand, where they got dried in almost no time.

Meanwhile the young adventurers had a bathe. Going over to the old quarry—a favourite place for a "dook"—all stripped and were soon paddling about like ducks. Sutherland was a fairly good swimmer, and had very little fear of the water.

An old boat was lying in the centre of the pool. He swam out to this and mounting on the gunwale gave a cheer, and dived in again. Some time passed, and there was no appearance of the lad. The others were beginning to be anxious. "A believe he's drooned," said Farquharson. This seemed to be the opinion of them all.

A cry for help was raised. People gathered round; some ran up to the farmhouse for ropes, &c.; others simply wrung their hands; the women cried. There was, in fact, a general hullabaloo. What was to be done? "Send for the police," suggested one. "The Humane Society," said another. "The Dock Commissioners," proposed a third.

At this point, Sutherland's head was seen to pop up from behind the side of the boat. There was no bottom in the thing, and he had been all the time quietly sitting on a seat inside, enjoying the grim joke he was playing.

After they had re-dressed they had a few races and some jumping contests which helped to pass the time. At length they made a start for the city, going round by Granton and Newhaven towards Leith. A stop was made at the Marine Parade, where they had another bathe, after which they made for home in earnest. They had overturned a wife's cherry barrow at Junction Bridge, and were convoyed half-way home by a crowd of Leith boys. A halt was made at the Ferry Road Toll, and after a good laugh each went his separate way home.

Classes and lessons had commenced again, and games and romps were once more running in their old grooves. Cricket was being zealously carried on in the seventh greens. The first eleven were practising hard for a match which had been arranged with a cricket club at Melrose, to which place the knaps were going in three weeks' time for their annual excursion.

The "'ird" greens having been restored to their normal condition, by the removal of all traces of the June Day erections, they were given up to the "bist" players. The game of football was, however, not so vigorously cultivated amongst the knaps. They had a knack of kicking each other's shins oftener than the ball. Whether they were "buckin' kickers" accidentally or intentionally it would be difficult to say; in any case it was only occasionally that the game was indulged in. The "'cond" greens were occupied by the small cricket clubs, of which there were many.

The principal junior club had a full set of five wickets, one bail, and a bat. The latter must have been made of some very peculiar wood. At this time it was like a bundle of splints, but it was still amongst the kids five years afterwards. The set of wickets and the bat were kept behind the door at the bottom of the "'cond" school stair, amongst a lot of other rubbish, which served its purpose too. Other kids' clubs of still less importance could not even boast of wickets. No matter; jackets were used, placed one around the other until the necessary pile was got; and many an interesting game was played in that way.

One evening after five o'clock one of Walter's friends, giving him a nudge in the ribs, inquired, "Are you gawn to bolt?"

"Where to?" asked Walter.

"Oh, no far, only ower to the kirkyaird to look for nests. I was ower the other nicht, and I ken twa or three rare nests—blackies' and mavis' and ony amount o' sparries'."

"Whae else is gawn?" queried Walter.

"Oh, there's Johnstone, and Sinclair, and Fraser, and Wilson, and yin or twa mair. We'll hae some rare fun. Sinclair kens whaur there's an auld skull lying, and he's gaun to nab it to mak' a locket o't. It mak's a far better yin than cocoanut-shell, and it rubs down as quick again. He wants yin fur the end o' a paip chain he's making. Wul ye come? Say yake or nay at yince, becus if no, I'm gawn to ask Swanston."

Walter did not care about the skull part of the business, but rather than be thought fud, he said "yake," that he would. They all gathered together at the green next to Greyfriars gate, and smooling down one at a time to the corner of the shrubs, away they bolted through the bushes.

ANDERSON'S TOMB.

Eventually all met at the corner of the wall which separates Greyfriars churchyard from the hospital grounds. Sinclair gave Johnstone a backie up on to the top of the dyke; Walter and the others followed in succession, Sinclair being pulled up last.

Getting over on the other side was an easy matter, as they had only to step on to a railing and jump into one of the enclosed portions. It was the last resting-place of Anderson of Kingask and his wife Janet.

A consultation was then held round the large stone sarcophagus which projects from the wall. The question was, What should be the next move? Sinclair advised going out one at a time, but as Johnstone said, "All the gravediggers and gardeners were awa hame to their 'pot,' and there wis naebody to be fud for but the deed yins, an' he wis shure they widna snitch ta Magnus." It was therefore agreed that all should go together.

Climbing over the railing and out of the private enclosure, they found themselves in the walk running up to the public way. Quietly stealing along this, as Sinclair said, "as much on the grass as possible," they passed through the arch into the churchyard proper. Sneaking up to the right, past some enclosed tombs, another wall was reached which had to be surmounted.

Climbing on to the railings which enclose the graves of the Moneypennys, and making a stepping-stone of the little carved emblem spades, a rake and a coffin crossed on each side of the gate posts, they mounted to the top of the wall, from which they dropped on to the soft mossy grass of the old and seldom-visited prison ground of the Covenanters.

Here everything was in a sadly neglected and forlorn-looking state. There was a feeling about it, more than about any other churchyard in Scotland, that it was in keeping with its long-forgotten dust. For the present, however, it was the happy hunting-ground of the knaps. The birds, no doubt, looked upon it as a place of absolute safety.

The walls were thickly overgrown with ivy. Dykes and old rusty railings separated the graves from the centre walk. The gates in many places had fallen from their fastenings, and little trees and bushes growing up between the bars fixed them to the ground with such firmness that nothing but the hatchet could ever free them. The very stone pillars spoke of times long past and gone; the elements having worn some of them to the very core. In some places the rank grass was growing to a height of two feet or more.

On dropping to the ground, the first thing which met Walter's gaze were a pair of large skulls and cross bones carved on the sides of one of the topmost gates. The sight made him feel rather queer; and the wish arose to be safely on the "Wark's" gravel again!

Wading down through the grass the first enclosure was ransacked. Here three nests were found, from which ten pretty little eggs were taken and carefully deposited in Sinclair's cap. On the way down, in the several tombs, a number more were got. Walter saw for the first time a nest with five little blue eggs spotted with black, snugly lying in their bed of soft feathers and down. This was one of the blackies' nests which his friend Ross had had under his eye for some time; now it was under his fingers.

A large number of eggs had now been secured; and it was time to think about returning. Making their way up to the gate, Sinclair stopped suddenly.

"Hist! what's that!" he said. All listened. Sure enough there was the tramp, tramp, of some one walking slowly up the gravel on the outside of the gate. "Hide! there's *sel*," quickly whispered Sinclair. Fortunately they were in front of an open gate. All slipped in except Johnstone who was too far down.

A figure was walking straight up to the gate. To throw himself flat among the tall grass was with Johnstone the work of an instant. Glancing up through the screen of grass in front of him, he saw old Brown, the sexton, looking steadily, and with evident suspicion, through the bars of the gate.

To make matters worse, the bell for the "learning" class pealed out loudly. Oh, what a quaking there was

COVENANTERS' PRISON.

in that old churchyard! Verily, a second set of Covenanters imprisoned. At every stroke of the bell their pluck seemed to fall down! down! down! until it got near to vanishing point.

Old Brown glared silently into the place. It was clear now that he thought something was wrong; or, judging by his vacant stare, perhaps he was only wondering if he would ever bury a *leevin'* soul in that place again. In any case he took his time and had his think out. The tiresome suspense to that little band and especially to Johnstone was awful. Talk about a martyrs' prison!

At length the old man was seen to take some keys from his pocket, and turning them over one by one on the string which held them together he picked out one with a very pleased grunt of satisfaction.

"Its a' up," whispered Johnstone. "We're a' nabb'd; a' better get up."

"No yet, no yet," hissed Sinclair. "Wait till I plank a' thir eggs."

Slowly old Brown put the key into the rusty padlock which held the gate. After trying for about five minutes he found it would not turn. Upon this he took another good dose of reflection and another long stare into the now darkening walk; then he turned and slowly walked away.

The boys lay quite still for a few minutes until the sound of the sexton's footsteps had died away. The first to speak was Johnstone.

"By hokey! wasn't that a narrow squeak?" said he.

"Amen" was the united reply.

Johnstone advised clearing out as quickly as possible, in case Brown should return with the proper key. Sinclair replaced his eggs in his hat and putting it on his head the boys made their way back to the walk through the churchyard, over the railings, and into Anderson's tomb. Johnstone was the last to get over. In the grey darkness he did not observe who was before him and in jumping off the dyke he placed his hand on Sinclair's head, to steady himself. Crack went all the eggs. Here was a nice mess.

"Oh! pot and plum-pud," groaned Sinclair, as he took off his cap, bending his head as schoolboys generally do when they have anything inside their cap besides their pate; and in truth the yolks and broken shells of twenty or thirty eggs were neither cleanly nor comfortable.

Sinclair's woful look was irresistible in the extreme. Even the place and circumstances had no control over the laughter of his companions. His rueful glance into the cap looking for the eggs was indeed comical, and his hair, as Johnstone remarked, amidst another burst of laughter, was a proper Heriot tartan.

If any of the masters had been on the other side of the wall, it would have struck them that a convivial party were enjoying themselves, instead of a number of their own lads on the straight road for punishment. The long grass was not so plentiful here, but enough was got together by his companions to shampoo Sinclair passably.

Climbing over the wall the little company dropped into the shrubbery. Now, in front of the reality, what was to be done? Johnstone's advice was to go right up to the "learning," and make a clean breast of it; but Sinclair, thinking no doubt of his appearance, counselled waiting until the bell rang. After all, they might not have been missed. This was accordingly agreed to as forming a possible loophole of escape.

They had about twenty minutes to wait, and sitting down at the back of the bushes they tried to feel as indifferent as possible. While they were seated, Smith asked if ever they had heard the story about the body snatchers and the garriers.

No one had heard the story, so Smith began in an appropriately low tone to tell it. The story was to this effect:

"A long time ago when the doctors used to buy the dead bodies, men often went into the Greyfriars kirkyard and dug up the bodies after they had been buried. Some o' the garriers hearing about it, and watching for themselves, saw how it was done.

"Generally there wis twa men. When they saw a funeral gawn into the kirkyard gate they followed and saw where the grave wis. At night they went in wi' a big pock and spades and dug a deep hole above the head and shouthers o' the body, and after breakin' the tap end o' the lid o' the coffin, they pu'd the body up out o' the hole. After takin' off the deid claes, which they flung doon the hole again, they popped the body into the bag. Then filling in the earth, and spreading the turf as neatly as possible, they shouthered the bag, and hooked it.

"The garriers made up their minds to play the snatchers a trick, so twa or three o' them went ower jist this same road we were the night an' waited where they were sure the hawks would come. The knap that was to play the principal part had a good long snab's awl in his pocket—yin o' yon sma thin yins, an' awfu' sherp.

"They hadna waited lang when up came twa men, and layin' down their coats they worked away like hatters and werna long in bringin' up the body. They gien him the sack, filled in the dirt, and then propin' the pock up against a heidstane, went away to hide their spades in the place where they usually put them. Now was the chance for the knaps, so getting a hud o' the big bundle they soon emptied the body out and had Puddin' Smith into the body's place, hurrying back into their hiding places, and hauling the body along wi' them.

"They were jist in time when back came the twa men. 'Gie me a bit hist up wi' it,' said the yin to the ither, and 'Puddin'' was landed on to the man's shouthers. 'Crickie! this is an awfu' heavy yin,' said he. 'I think he's deed wi' eating ower much.' This was all that was said until they reached the dyke at Candlemakers' Raw, when the bag was laid down.

"The garriers had been creeping at the back of them a' the time, and could hear fine onything that was said. The one says to the other, 'Man I think this yin hasna been lang deid, for he is gey warm yet, an' guessin' by his weight, he mun hae been an awfu' chap for his kail.' Jumpin' ower the dyke, the yin handed, or rather shoved, the bag ower to the ither, and it came down on the grund wi' a thud that garr'd 'Puddin'' grunt. 'Did you hear that?' said the one. 'Aye,' said the other, 'that's the wind left in the stamick, ave heard it often.' Sure enough, thought Smith, an' ye'll hear it again shortly. They took a rest for a minute or twa on the ither side of the dyke, and then the bag was histed on the man's back again. 'Which way now?' says he, 'down the Raw or up Bristy Port?' 'Down the Raw,' shouted 'Puddin',' and at the same time he shoved the shoemaker's awl into the man's trousers with an awfu' penetrating vengeance that made him drap Puddin' like a plate o' hot 'pot' on the causey. The rest o' the garriers jumping ower the dyke at the same time, the twa men thought it wis Auld Nick and his angels coming after them, an' they bolted like lightning."

Such was Smith's story. Just as he had finished, the bell rang. The different classes had been released; and some of the boys running down to the well for a drink it was an easy matter for the adventurers to mingle with them. Very soon they found their way into the square, where they learned that they had not been missed. In short they were "clear," and the only thing to be done now was to get to bed and "stick in" to their lessons in the morning.

The weather was intensely warm, and as a reward for good conduct among the boys in general a promise had been made that they would be taken down to "Portie" for an afternoon's bathing. Accordingly, everyone had been on his best behaviour, so that Dr Bedford with his kindly smile, which he always wore when he was communicating anything agreeable to the boys, announced his intention of going with them to Portobello that afternoon. A lusty cheer followed the announcement.

All ran gleefully to their separate classes, where, we may be sure, they got their tasks off all the better in anticipation of the coming treat. This day, like the others, was extremely warm—just such a day as the enthusiastic juvenile bather rejoices in. Certainly it was rather a long walk from the "Wark" to Portobello to be undertaken in such broiling weather; but who thought of the length of the road when a dip in the sea was to come at the end of it?

When the time arrived for starting, all were marshalled and formed into fours. Then off they went, with towels in their pockets, through the Greyfriars walk. As they passed through the second gate, Sinclair nudged Walter. "Do you mind auld Brown?" Walter shuddered a little. Well did he remember auld Brown and all the other incidents of that evening! Their way led up Greyfriars Place, Bristo Port, Lothian Street, Drummond Street, and Back

Canongate. Very soon they reached the Queen's Park, the little fellows trudging on bravely, boasting of their aquatic powers and long-distance swimming abilities. On the Portobello road "Pud" Tod could do sixty strokes; but when Walter observed him in the sea he noted that he could only do about five with his head under water, and that without progressing one inch.

As they passed the gate leading out of the Park, a big cairn on the left received an addition of some two hundred stones. The cairn was said to have been piled over a murderer; at anyrate it was certainly growing larger. What its dimensions would ultimately have been if the knaps had passed it often may be readily guessed.

A good mile of road had yet to be covered before the sea would be reached, but already many of the boys were untying their boots, so eager were they to be in the water.

The first sight of the waves was greeted with expressions of the keenest delight by the boys. They had just reached the brick-work, from which a good view of the beach is obtained. And who, on going there to enjoy the water, has not been charmed with the sight of the long curling waves which roll gracefully up on to the shining sands, their fleecy tops glancing in the bright sunshine, inviting even those who had been without any such intention to plunge in and try? To be sure you are not long in these grand big feathery waves before you find that they carry with them a somewhat uncomfortable quantity of cinders and other waste substances.

Nevertheless, cinders and all, the boys thought it jolly enough. The knaps stripped on the green park which stretches a long way continuous with the beach, and scampering down the sands they soon had the water alive, laughing, screaming, and playing their pranks on one another. The Doctor enjoyed the scene immensely, and Levick was everywhere with his wise sayings.

One boy made a great dive into a huge wave, but the wave receded at the moment, and he plunged on to a quantity of cinders, &c., which it had left behind. It did hurt too, but a little careful washing removed all the pieces. A race along the beach at length made a finish to a splendid bathe and some rare fun.

The march back was by way of Duddingston Road, when the company got a drink at the village pump, the "cheer" of the "Sheep's Head" tavern being too expensive for the knaps. A rest on the brae facing Duddingston Loch was much appreciated and enjoyed.

By the time the "Wark" was reached there were some very tired little travellers; and the rapidity with which the "doses" disappeared indicated that there were some very hungry ones too.

CHAPTER VII.

CAUTIOUS confabs were going on amongst the lawds and cholds. Something was clearly in the wind. Little pieces of rope, it was noticed, were being rolled into hard "couts," applied with great vigour to the pillars, and then minutely examined, pulled and pinched until they were both hard and tight. What was the reason for so many arming themselves in this way? That was the inquiry, which was answered with a "Wheesht, quiet," and then the "couts" were packed away into the pockets of their owners.

It was Saturday morning, and on leaving the square a number of the older boys were found waiting by the little stone pillar at the corner of the building, on the outside, opposite the council room window. They stopped one or two of each batch of knaps as they passed out, and after they had whispered something to them, they also waited behind. Some thirty or forty having been selected in this way, a start was made.

Passing out at the gate, about a dozen were posted at Wharton Lane; the same number took their stand at the Meadow Poles; while the remainder kept watch on the front entrances of Watson's Hospital.

The "neets" coming up unsuspectingly were quickly pounced upon by the angry knaps, whereupon they retreated into their school grounds. Out of these grounds no inducement or challenge would make them venture. The full strength of the George Watson's boys being eighty, and the Heriots just one hundred more, the Watsons could hardly know what the outside strength might be.

After a considerable wait, a cry was heard from the Meadow Poles direction. It was evident that the battle had begun on the left flank. The Meadow Walk division having surprised a sortie leaving by a door on that side of the wall, the knaps gave chase and fairly routed the enemy. Some of the "neets," thinking that the main body were engaged in that place, ran back and tried to force an exit by the central gate.

At this point a general hunt began. As a last resource the remainder of the besieged made for the Wharton Lane gate, but here also they were trapped and followed with crushing effect.

By this time nearly all the "neets" were out, and chasing and fighting was going on in every direction. The affair was really assuming alarming proportions. At the corner of Forrest Road a good "bicker" was engaged in between Buff Simpson and one of the principal offenders amongst the "neets." Simpson being a strong and rather ferocious fellow would have doubtless, if he had not been stopped, made sad havoc of his man.

Matters were getting really serious. In almost every street in the locality, scrimmages were taking place. Even as far as the Lawnmarket, where a close leads down to the Mound, some of the "neets" were chased. They had to take refuge in a small swill-shop, where they were kept until relieved by some of their friends.

The Meadows were occupied as a field of operations, but there the knaps had rather the worst of it. By a clean trick, or rather by a good bit of generalship, the "neets" allowed a number of the knaps to come on, and suddenly halting, turned, showed fight, and gave the venturesome knaps a fine drubbing.

Someone had in the meantime informed Dr Bedford of the state of matters, and the Doctor now sent out the wardsmen and other officials who were about the place. Affairs had not altogether quietened down until about two o'clock, when the last of the avengers pocketed their "couts," and went home satisfied with their revenge for the attack of June Day.

At night all were in and full of talk about their success, and went to their evening devotions never suspecting that anything would be said about the forenoon's proceedings. They were seated in the Chapel and the Doctor stalked in. The usual reading, praise and prayer had been gone through and Dr Bedford came down from the pulpit.

He stepped in front of the precentor's box, and putting his hands behind his back looked all round at the boys for a minute or so. They knew very well by this that something was coming. Dr Bedford's face wore a serious and vexed expression; stepping astride until his feet were about a yard apart (a fashion the Doctor often had when speaking to the boys; perhaps he thought the movement brought him more down to their level, he being in height fully six feet), at length he spoke—" Would the boys who were concerned in the disgraceful affair with the Watson lads to-day stay behind." Presently he made the usual motion for them to rise and march out. All got to their feet and turned towards the door except those who were bold enough to own up to their conduct.

When all had retired who meant to do so, the Doctor ordered the warder to close the inside doors. The first three forms and one or two here and there all over the Chapel, even down to the youngest seats, were filled with delinquents to the number of about fifty.

The Doctor scanned them closely and then motioned the others to come to the seats occupied by the eldest boys. They did as they were asked, and the Doctor, whose face had now a brighter look, began—"Well boys, if you misbehave yourselves, you also know how to be truthful. I know nearly every boy who was concerned in this disturbance of to-day."

As he spoke, a couple of rats, thinking it time that they had the sole use of the Chapel, were observed sporting at the other end. This was too much for some of the youngsters, and a rush was made at the rodents, who, however, got down the grating out of danger in a moment.

The boys resumed their seats and quiet was restored. "Was anyone prepared to give an explanation of to-day's behaviour"? inquired the Doctor. Upon this one of the elder boys, nick-named Dandou, rose up, and told the story of June Day. The Doctor's reply was not reassuring: However great their grievance, he said, or under whatever circumstances, they had no right to take the punishment into their own hands. They should have complained to him and he would have had the matter put right in a proper manner.

The most objectionable feature in the whole affair was its premeditation. If it had been simply an accidental fray, he might have passed it over; as it was, he felt bound to hold a court-martial, and punish accordingly. He hoped that the same honesty which had made all those concerned remain behind, would prompt the principals to confess, and so lighten his disagreeable duty. In any case all would have to attend a special Court to be held on Saturday morning.

Several of Walter's friends, as well as Walter himself, had been concerned in the business. When they got to their ward and into bed there was, of course, much talk about all that had occurred.

One of the boys asked if they had ever heard the story of the "bat" with the Colinton folks. Some replied that they had, but the majority cried "Go on." So the story proceeded somewhat as follows:

"Not long ago a number of the knaps went out to Colinton purposely to see the Snuff Mills. After their curiosity had been satisfied and they were coming through the village, the Colinton boys, like others, thought to molest them. A bicker was the result, and the knaps were roughly handled.

"On arriving at the Wark a complaint was made to the lawds, and the very next day about four or five and twenty mustered and marched out to Colinton. They left their capes at a cottage on the road side as they went along, and putting on the war paint, commenced operations. The first move was to make little bings of stones at regular intervals by the way. These were to serve as ammunition in case they should have to retreat.

"Just as they reached the village they met their enemies, and a stiff fight ensued. The village boys at first took refuge in the smithy, but the blacksmith was glad to run them out. After that they took to the school-room, but the windows were smashed to pieces. The fight waxed furious, backwards and forwards on the road and in the fields. In the end the knaps were victorious, and with their handkerchiefs flying from branches of trees, they marched to the cottage where they had left their capes. Here a collection was made for the wife's bairns; and a triumphal march was then made into town." Such was the story of the Colinton " bat."

A COURT-MARTIAL.

On Saturday morning the Court was held in the seventh school or lecture room, a long room on the north side of the square. The floor sloped upwards, and the raised desks and seats formed a gallery capable of holding about one hundred boys. The gallery on this occasion was filled with onlookers. In the body of the room sat the culprits.

Dr Bedford took his place at Billie's desk, armed and prepared to dispense cane justice. Some of the minor offences were disposed of before the case of the riot was taken up. Here is part of the list :—

- CASE FIRST.—Charged with throwing stones, or gravel, at the carving above the Chapel door. Defence: That he was trying for a doufed ball. Punishment: Six stripes and one hour's confinement, with a recommendation not to try the same thing again.
- CASE SECOND.—Charged with being found in the shrubbery. Defence: Looking for a lost ball. Punishment: Six stripes and a caution not to lose balls there.
- CASE THIRD.—Murray and Tod. Charged with giving impertinence to one of the wardsmen, and furthermore daring to call him a porter. Found guilty. Sentence: Solitary confinement for four hours, and, as a task, to write out a copy of twelve pages. First six sheets to contain (in small hand) the text, "Honour and obey those in command;" the other six sheets to contain, "Bless the hand that punishes for offence." [It was well that in this case the copies were not revised, otherwise the consequences might have been serious.]

Several other little cases were disposed of in a similar manner.

In calling the case for riot, the Doctor explained that he was so pleased with the truthfulness of the boys, and the manly spirit in which all had come forward, that he would deal leniently with the offenders, but he should like to impress upon them that if such a scene occurred again, they would be dealt with in a most rigorous manner. He was determined to stamp out all disgraceful occurrences, and he hoped that the boys would profit by his leniency.

The ten eldest were then called. They were rewarded with two hours' confinement. The next ten got one hour; while the remainder received three strokes of the cane.

As ten strokes of Dr Bedford's cane were just about equal to one from any of the other masters, the last set of culprits got off very easily.

The time for the excursion was now drawing near. "This is Wednesday," said Ross, "tomorrow's Thursday, and we'll get out in the afternoon to bring in some sock and bakes. Then, hurrah! the next day's the excursion."

These remarks were wound up by a twirl of the speaker's Glengarry bonnet, which, by the way, he had transformed into a Balmoral by damping and pulling out the edges and thus altering the shape. The bonnet whirled up past the first millar, and was deftly caught upon the owner's head, greatly to his own satisfaction and the wonder of those around.

"You could not do that again," said one of the knaps to Ross. Ross would not try; one success was sufficient: if he tried again he might "dirk" it.

The question arose—What are you gawn to bring in? One was going to Croll's in Hanover Street, where he could get "a big coco-nit for fourpence, and a rare fig-cake for ither thrym';" and what with "bakes, sock and lemonade," he was "gawn to spend about twa-an'-six"; that was between him and Simpson, as they were "gethering up thegither and we're chums-a wi' everything."

"Are you gawn to hae a fishing basket?" asked Ross. "'Yake,' we're gawn to hae yin each, and I'll take twa bottles for water; we'll hae some rare fizzers wi' tartar, baking-soda and sugar. I had some rare stuff last excursion: dae ye mind, Dixon? I was gien' you a drink at the station just as Harvey was killed."

"What way was he killed?" queried Walter.

"O, Daddie Wight's horse bolted, and he was knocked down and run ower. It stopped a' oor fun that day, an' we were a' gushin' for his folk."

"Let's hope there'll be nae accidents this time," was Ross' remark.

It was getting dusky and the swallows were beginning to whirl round and round the square. As the knaps said, they were playing at cross-tig, and a good half-hour's fun was got "trying" for them with their bonnets which they threw up amidst the whirling birds.

All round the rhones on the leads were carved figures with grotesque gaping mouths. Each of these was taken up with a family of swallows; and a glorious time they had of it flying round in circles, the whistling sometimes being continuous. Curiously enough, the same figures on the outside, facing the greens, were mostly taken up by the "Dakies" or crows—"Meenie's Dakies," as they were termed, no doubt because Meenie used to put out crusts or "crockles" to feed them.

On the afternoon the boys got home for their provisions, although it was preferred that they should not bring anything more than a few sweets and biscuits, as the extra supplies interfered with the large quantity of lamb sandwiches and milk which were provided for the boys.

However, each as he came in had either a fishing basket or a courier bag well filled with the usual confectionery, purchased by boys when in possession of high spirits and a few coppers. Nearly every one had the almost indispensable "cocoa-nut, fig-cake, and sherbit," some in small, others in large quantities. There were "bakes," "katieflips," "jib," and big pandrops, lemonade and ginger-beer. If not for what was in them, the bottles were useful for holding water to drink when in the train.

"Are you gawn to keep waken a' night?" said Ross to Walter. "If you like," was the reply. "Maist o' the knaps in the ward are gawn to," said Ross. When they were in bed the usual round of stories was told, and a few coups were perpetrated, but before long all had fallen sound asleep.

Next morning Walter was dreaming of being out at Hailes quarry gathering brambles. His hold slipped, and he was tumbling down—down—and never coming to the bottom. As the loose rocks and stones were rolling with him, thundering down the sides of the quarry, he awoke. What was that most unusual noise which saluted his ears? He held on to his mattress like grim death. "Help! help!" he was heard crying. At this moment a hearty cheer resounded through the square, and there came a sound as if the artillery were firing a volley there. What was it? The cry then got up, "Daddie Wight; it's Daddie Wight."

And there, sure enough, was Daddie's cart and his great grey horse, rattling and stamping in the square. In a minute or two all the windows of the govies', 'coud, and other wards were filled with yelling boys, every one in his "chalker."

Ross explained to Walter that Wight's was the only cart that came into the square all the year. It certainly made up for many others in noise.

No more of bed for the knaps now. All were busy brushing boots, washing, and otherwise preparing for the long anticipated day's outing.

When the bell rang all were ready to go downstairs; and, after partaking of a slight refreshment, they were ranged round the quadrangle. There they were, with baskets and bags and fishing rods, their faces eager with excitement and expectation.

In front was the band, the players with their white vests and yellow cap-bands, and the brass instruments shining like gold.

At this point, the worthy Doctor stepped into the centre of the square. In a few words he cautioned the boys to be careful and not get into harm's way. The band, he likewise said, were to cease playing when they reached the station.

The order "U-Re! form fours, right face, forward!" from Magnus, brought the band into play. The tune was that favourite quick-step, commonly called "Boyne Water," and right merrily it went. A number of friends and relatives of the boys were gathered at the gate to escort them down to the station and wish them a pleasant day. On reaching Bank Street, the tune was changed to "Cheer, Boys, Cheer," the band continuing to play until the arrival of the company at the station.

In a very short time all were safely packed into the "special" for Melrose, each carriage having in it a wardsman, master, or responsible monitor, who, as the train whirled along, pointed out the places of historic interest. Walter, Ross, Sinclair, Toby, Tindal and a few others had managed to get into the same compartment. Cockie, being the teacher in charge, gave them an interesting account of the different towers and castles which they passed. After disposing of several bottles of lemonade and other good things which they had with them, they became very jolly. The scenery in the beautiful valley of the Tweed through which they were passing greatly delighted them.

The river with its many windings and lovely rippling streams, was quite in accordance with the spirits of the delighted boys, and Toby, while cheering to some of the cottagers, brought his head into the carriage minus his hat. This was great fun for the knaps, though it was no fun for Toby. However, his red handkerchief, tied at the four corners, made a very convenient substitute, as the day was extremely hot.

On arrival at Melrose Station, the company was drawn up four deep, and, with the band in front playing "See the Conquering Hero Comes," they were taken down to the Town Hall—the rendezvous for the day—where all articles that were unnecessary for the forenoon's enjoyment were left.

The fishers armed themselves with their rods and creels, while the eleven who were to play the cricket match, shouldering their stumps, bats, and pads, &c., went off to the ground for an hour's practice in view of the approaching contest.

Crighton and his chums followed Cockie to the Abbey, where they were shown the tombs of more than one great Scotsman. Leaving the Abbey, our friends followed some of the company *en route* to the Tweed. As they approached the river, the first thing that attracted their attention was the high swinging bridge which crosses it at this point. When they got to the centre, the bridge was made to swing in a manner that really made Walter wonder it did not topple over altogether.

On reaching the other side, they turned up to the left, and found themselves amongst clumps of huge marguerites and other wild flowers which here lined the banks in the most beautiful profusion. The colours harmonising so nicely with the sparkling waters of the Tweed as they glittered and danced in the sunshine, made, as one of the teachers remarked, a sight "well worth remembering." Wandering up the banks they came upon what Ross called a grand bit for a "dook." The suggestion was enough; in a moment or two all had stripped and were floundering about like young porpoises. Everything went on blithely until one of the party got into a hole and was nearly drowned. By the united efforts of two others he was drawn to the side more dead than alive. This incident put a stop to the bathing, and every boy got dressed as quickly as possible

In a short time all were restored to their usual good humour, except a few of the keen anglers, who were wroth with the bathers for having entirely frightened the fish. Perhaps the bathing was merely put forward as an excuse for their non-success.

Retracing their steps, the company soon arrived at the Town Hall, where a number were waiting until dinner should be served. The cricket team went off to the match under the charge of Billie; others either followed the game or took a stroll to Abbotsford, or went once more to the river.

Walter and his set chose to survey the small "sock" shops and quaint-looking old houses of the place, managing, of course, to spend some of their odd coppers in the former.

The afternoon passed quickly, and as the time for departure drew near, there arrived from the cricket field a victorious eleven, who had won by 38 runs and 2 wickets to fall.

Before leaving Melrose another supply of bread and milk was handed round, over which the events of the day were discussed.

The fishing rods had not accomplished much. Indeed, the only evidence which Walter had of fish being in the river was one little yellow trout, about four inches long, which was being triumphantly exhibited by one of the Doctor's family.

The band gave the natives a few selections from their somewhat limited *répertoire*—" O Where, Tell Me Where" and " The British Grenadiers" being amongst the number. At length the train steamed away amidst the ringing cheers of the people.

On reaching the Waverley Station, a crowd of the parents and friends of the knaps were found waiting their arrival. After being formed, the boys marched up by Bank Street, and the band struck up " Slap, Bang, Here we are again," keeping up their music until the " Wark" was reached, into which the youngsters turned, tired and sleepy, having thoroughly enjoyed themselves.

CHAPTER VIII.

NEXT morning being Saturday, Walter went home, and was able to tell his mother and sisters some wonderful stories about Melrose. At noon, Ross and Sinclair called to see if he would go to Pinkie pier for a bathe, and Walter being agreeable the three set off together.

On the way down by Princes Street they met with Johnstone and a little fellow, named Crick, who both joined the company. Johnstone had saved some coppers from the day before, and was open to lay them out on "sock" or such like.

"What do you say to a smoke?" was Sinclair's suggestion.

"What kind of a smoke?" inquired Johnstone.

"Buy a pipe and baccy, of course."

Ross and Walter concurred, but little Crick thought it would be better to spend the "maiks" on toffee or "jib." Crick was, however, in the minority, and so the pipe and the twist were duly secured.

About half-way down Leith Walk, on the west side, there was a piece of vacant ground fronting some little cottages. Here they squatted themselves on the grass. Sinclair proved a good hand at pipe-filling. Taking the first turn, and the tobacco being fresh and ill to kindle, he was almost the colour of the clay before the pipe was thoroughly alight. Johnstone had the next "pull." He puffed away in great clouds for about a minute; then he handed the emblem of peace to Ross, who in turn gave it to Walter. Even little Crick made an attempt, but he managed to swallow the first mouthful and could not be prevailed upon to try again.

By this time all were lying flat on the grass, not one daring to lift his head for fear that the other should see how the first smoke had "done" for him. Sick and helpless, there they were, and there they lay for about a quarter of an hour. At last Walter got up, with the remark that he did not think he would try it again: a resolution in which the rest readily joined. Ross, in fact, proposed to pitch the pipe and tobacco over the railings, but, after thinking the matter over, it was agreed to give the weed away to someone who could use it. On getting up to the pavement, the first one they met was a baker, board on head.

"Do you smoke?" asked Ross.

"Aye," said the baker.

Would he then accept this pipe and tobacco?

"Oh aye," answered the man, with a knowing grin, as he looked at the pale faces of the boys.

There was not much talk on the way down. Entering Leith Docks, they made their way round to Pinkie pier. The tide being full in, only a swimmer could enter the water, and as they could all do a little in that way except Crick they had soon plunged in, and were paddling along the bulwarks. While swimming too close in, an unfortunate accident happened to Walter: he struck his leg on the side of the pier, and a shell or some such thing cut an ugly gash on the top of his knee. The wound bled a great deal, but Walter managed to staunch the flow by tying his pocket handkerchief tightly round his leg. The cut was, indeed, more severe than they at first thought, for it was with difficulty that Walter managed to walk back to town. Nothing, however, was said about it, either at home or in the " Wark," and after a day or two the knee was all right again.

Walter's " Wark " jacket, or what we may term his every-day jacket, was getting rather shabby. Accordingly, he was ordered by Magnus to go to the " Bells " * and get a change.

"THE BELLS."

* The "Bells" was a small apartment in which was stored a miscellaneous collection of the knaps' old clothes and boots which had been patched up in a manner more distinguished for strength than neatness. It resembled in many ways the old clothes shops which used to be such a feature of the meaner streets of the Old Town, and particularly in the disposal of misfits, as is usual in such circumstances, all the little knaps getting jackets or trousers distinctly providing for immediate and exuberant growth, and the big knaps being handed garments which, as the old Jewish dealer said, fitted them "like ze paper on ze wall."

Next morning, therefore, about half-past eight, he, along with nine or ten others, all requiring a "shift" of some part of their clothing, congregated at the "Bells" door. This store was situated on the first floor of the north-west wing, next to the wifies' rooms. One of the wardsmen coming upstairs opened the door, the top panel of which was made of obscured glass. It was a long strip of a room, fitted all round with shelves, packed with repaired clothing. The first boy on the line wanted a jacket, but there not being one of his own in stock he had thrown at him the next which fitted him best, his old one being pitched into the pile which awaited the attention of the tailor. The next boy required a vest; and so on, until all the various wants were supplied.

Matters went on very quietly for a time; and as the July examinations and holidays were approaching, both teachers and pupils were making hard endeavours to have their classes and lessons well up.

With the younger boys everything was easy enough in any case, so that the extra spurt did not make much difference to them. Every day was taken up with revisals. Walter could repeat many of his lessons by heart, such as "Androcles and the Lion," "Big Claus and Wee Claus," and many other stories and fables which were interesting, and therefore easily learned. He had also a good knowledge of the map of the world, and of Scotland; while in simple addition, multiplication and subtraction, he was fairly well up. These, along with the multiplication table, were the extent of his section's curriculum.

One morning, on passing the door at the bottom of the sixth school stair, Walter was "collared" by Ross and Johnstone. "Hullo, Crighton, where are you gaun?"

"A'm gawn up to Fummie for a needle an' thread, as I want to sew on a button or twa."

"Good," said Ross, "get plenty o' thread, an' I'll take the len o' the needle after you."

"A' right," cried Walter; "A'm chums-a'."

He was moving away quickly when Ross cried, "Here, Wattie."

"Aye, what is't?"

He came back, and Ross looked all round to be sure that no one was listening.

"See here," he said, "are you on fur a feed o' strawberries the nicht?"

"Yes," said Walter, "but where are we to get them?"

A whisper in Walter's ear was the reply. Walter nodded his head. "A' richt," he said, "I'll see you after in the hall."

Ross and Johnstone proceeded to the store, on a message for the cook, returning with a tub of stores, almost too heavy to be carried between them. Both received for their trouble a good slice of bread and butter from the cook.

The day's tasks had been got over; and with a game of "swipie" in the "'cond" greens the evening passed very pleasantly until time for "pot." After that, Ross, Johnstone, Walter, and other two met together outside the pend gate. By good luck, the evening was rather dull, which greatly favoured the escapade; if it had been fine they were sure to have been observed from some of the windows which overlooked the gardens. The question was whether to enter by climbing the wall inside the shed gate, or to go by the shrubbery. After a little discussion it was agreed to "gang doon the shrubs." On reaching the gate leading to the shed, they made a "shape" as if they were going in there, but instead bolted down through the bushes, along the walk to where the Doctor's garden wall joined that of the Heriot Bridge School. Over this they soon scrambled, and found themselves at once among the Doctor's preserves, among the cabbages, the carrots, and the other vegetable produce intended for the use of the Doctor's own household. Over in that corner, now empty, there had once flourished a goodly quantity of rhubarb, which had furnished the knaps with many an excellent gumstick. However, the strawberries were the temptation now. Creeping along by the foot of the garden, a little more than midway they came to about twenty rows of strawberry plants, growing up the sloping bank, at the top of which was the bowling or croquet green.

Quietly they crept along and up the rows, picking the delicious fruit, and eating as fast as possible.

"Hist!" was the exclamation that came from Johnstone. All were down flat in an instant.

"What is it?" whispered Ross.

"Don't pick them all," was the reply; "leave one here and there, and they will never know."

"All right," came the answer, and on they went as before. Walter had just reached the stage of thinking that a little sugar would be an improvement when the clank of a closing door struck upon his ear.

"Follow me, quickly," whispered Johnstone, and all made the bolt back by the road they had come. There was just time and no more to hide themselves; some behind a pile of old forcing frames which had been put up against the wall, others behind a heap of manure. All were quite still in a twinkling. The footfalls came straight down the walk at the side of which they lay hiding. How their hearts did beat when they saw old Peter, the gardener. Peter, however, passed on. He was simply going to shut one of the little hot-house boxes, the lid of which had been left open. He had been frightened for the night air, and had come back to make sure. Giving a general look round, he stuck his hands behind his back and quietly strolled up the walk again. For a time none of the adventurers dared almost breathe; nor did one of them speak until after the door was shut, and Peter had got time to be well away. Ross, popping his head out from the back of the frames, gave a heavy sigh.

"Ah, wisn't that gey near it?"

Johnstone assented, looking uncommonly serious.

"It wisna like Peter," he said; "however, we've done him for yince."

"Aye," struck in Walter, "we may thank our stars, and get back to the Wark again."

Mounting the wall, they all dropped down on the other side. Alas! they had no sooner landed than everyone of them was caught except Tamsin, who gave a jink and bolted up the shrubbery.

"Aye; Johnstone, Ross, Crighton, Pearson." said Jamie the warder, "what's this you've been after?" Two of the warders and old Peter were standing round the cowering knaps.

"We've been dae'n naething," said Ross."

"Naething!" exclaimed Peter, with a sneer. "Dae ye ca' robbing the garden o' fruits and vegetables naething?"

As he spoke he put his hand under Johnstone's jacket and pulled out a splendid specimen of the home-grown carrot. "Dae ye ca' that naething? I'm bound to say it didna grow under your coat onyway." This last remark evidently came from seeing the look of apparent wonder with which Johnstone surveyed the carrot and his jacket pocket. "Aye, an' ye thought ye had done me, did ye? Dinna try it lads; this system of robbery maun be put a stop to, somehow or anither."

"Who was the other boy?" asked Jamie.

"CAUGHT."

Every one was silent.

"Very well, perhaps you will tell when we get up to the lodge. Come along."

And so away they went, Ross quietly getting rid of a carrot amongst the bushes as he passed. On entering the square, the boys were told to go to their places. As bad luck would have it, one of the teachers was on duty, so that he would have to attend to the offenders.

When the service was over, and the master had descended to the front of the pulpit, a slip was handed to him by the warder. When he had read it, he called out—"Ross, Johnstone, Pearson, and Crighton, all go over to the lodge; and the other boy who was in their company go over too. His name is known, so he may as well go; if not, he will be doubly punished to-morrow."

The boys were then dismissed, and a little group congregated round the culprits, inquiring eagerly as to what they had been doing. The lads were, however, too much put about to say anything.

"Well, he canna kill you fur't onyway"—this was their consolation from the other side. Tamsin asked Ross and Walter if he should come over.

"Just as you like," said Ross. "A wadna if a wis you. A dinna believe he kens that you wis there."

"Ach!" ejaculated Johnstone, "it's jist a try on o' that sneak, Jamie. You gang away up to your ward, and we'll see how we get on."

"A richt," said Tamsin, "but if he's gaun to pin you for no telling, just say it wis me."

They went straight across the square and into the lodge. Turning into a little room, they took up their places in front of the table and waited for the inevitable. The summary punishments given here were various. For minor offences, one or two stripes; for other offences, more stripes—perhaps six or eight. If the offence were of an aggravating character it was a case of "touch your toes," which meant a spring with each whack that made you jump almost as high as your own head. If the misdemeanour were of a very serious nature the punishment was by hokey.

In this case the table was brought into requisition. The entertainment was generally supplied by the House Governor, with a cane for a conjuring apparatus.

Six or eight stripes, when a skilled and practised arm applied them, were terrible enough in their way, especially in cold weather, when perhaps there was no chance to "warm" for them. But with a green-horn of a master, an adept at the business could, by "shoving in," get the full force of the stroke on the cuff of his coat, and with tremendous squeezing, a show of pain, yelling and wetting his eyes with saliva, make the teacher think he was leaving a lasting impression, when in reality the boy was almost like to die of laughing.

But to return. Our delinquents on the present occasion stood quietly awaiting the entrance of the Wee-Dig, who was the teacher on duty. Their glances rested on the different articles in the room, from the bell rope, which hung behind the door, to the canary roosting on its perch at the window, which I have no doubt they envied in its innocence. However, there was nothing else for it but to gleefully rub their hands in preparation for what they were sure to get. (If an auld callant, no matter how long he had been away from the old "Wark," were to enter the lodge, the first thing he would likely do would be to rub his hands!)

"Oh, murder, here he comes," was the mental exclamation. And in he did come, with his black cloak hanging down his back, it having slipped from his shoulders. He had his teeth shut together, which gave his high cheek bones extra prominence, and, being naturally dark and swarthy, he now looked more than usually fierce. But we must give him his due. He was not a bad fellow at all; only he did wear a fierce expression; in the dim light of the lodge a redskin warrior, done up for the occasion as a dominie, could not have been more terror-striking.

Closing the door and turning to the boys, he inquired—"Well, what have you to say for yourselves?"

None of them spoke, but they all kept rubbing their hands as a preparation for the inevitable.

"Come, answer me: what were you doing over the wall?"

"Looking for a ball which was knocked over," answered Ross.

"Does it take five boys to look for one ball which has been knocked over the wall?" he asked.

"Sometimes," put in Johnstone.

The master looked hard at him, but evidently thought this too well answered to take any notice of it. "Aye! And did you find the ball?"

"No, sir; we ha'dna time," said Pearson, thinking that matters were getting hopeful—that, in fact, a distant shadow of acquittal was becoming apparent.

"But, sir," slyly broke in the warder, "they had plenty of time to eat strawberries, and pull carrots," holding up the prime root taken from Johnstone as a sample and condemnatory evidence. A slight pause followed, and the boys again commenced rubbing.

"Aye, aye: everything is clear enough," said the master. "You have pilfered the fruit and vegetables; now I'll give you the dessert." Having said which, he unrolled his tawse, and the delinquents had a good round half-dozen stripes each. "Now, who was the other boy?" queried the master. The only answer was a lengthened pause.

"Well, since he is not here to have his share, you shall have it amongst you." "Up again," and round went another half-dozen. As he finished his last stroke he remarked rather breathlessly that if ever they were found at anything of the kind again the punishment would not be so light. Picking up their caps all made haste outside and upstairs.

As they entered the ward, many a compassionate glance was bestowed upon the teared-stained faces of Walter and his companions. They knelt down in front of their little stools and said prayers, then quietly retired to rest. All the lights were lowered, and Levick retired.

"I say, how many did you get?" said one of the boys to Ross.

"Twelve," was the reply.

"And he wid lay it on, too," said another.

Here one of the smaller fellows cried out—"I ken wha telt on you."

At this all ears were open.

"Whae?" was the half-gasped inquiry from about twenty voices.

"Wee Clerk telt me that he heard Skin telling Jamie the porter, that when he wis hiding behind the sixth school stair door, he had heard Ross and Johnstone makin' it up to ask Crighton to gang wi' them, so it's jist been him that put *sel'* on your track."

"The tawnying sumph o' a teller, he deserves a proper muggin'," said one.

"What do you say to make a flee-on?" remarked another.

"He'll get another snaw hoose onyway," added a third.

Of course Armstrong would hear about it in the morning. One of the story-tellers now volunteered his services with a short tale about a "dug" that once belonged to the "Wark," but before he got one sentence out, about a dozen of "bowsters" and several hair-brush bags, &c., were thrown at his head. "Shut up, you and your dug; we dinna want to hear that story for about the five-hundredth time; it's time you were hanged like the dug."

"There's a good story though about some knaps that went to nab yaps in yin o' the gardens ower at Bruntsfield," said one.

"Let's hear it," cried all.

"Oh, there's no very much about it, but jist the way the gardener wis done.

"Twa or three o' the knaps used to bolt, and get rare pouchfuls o' fruit in a garden that wis up at the back o' where Leven Street is now. They would gang ower by the dyke at the links yonder; it's away now though. The man that the place belonged to set a watch yae nicht, and jist as they had got plenty, he made a dive for them, but only collared yae knap. It wis dark, and of course he couldna see him right, so he quietly cut off the second lowest button o' his jacket and then let him off. But the knaps were as fly as him, an' when they got back to the Wark they garr'd every yin cut off the same button.

"Next morning after their 'pot' they were a' telt to fall in in the square, and the gardener, walking into the middle, wis asked to pick out the yin he wis wanting. So, pointing out the knap he thought likest, he wis asked to come out. Catching up the corner o' the knap's jacket he triumphantly placed the button on the place where he had cut it off.

"'Is that him!' asked the Govie.

"'There's nae mistake,' said Cabbages, with a wink and a grin. 'Look! there's whaur I cut the button off, an' there's the button itsel'.'

"The knap swore black wis blue, that he never had been there, and as the Govie kent he couldna be, he asked the gardener to try another. 'Aweel, you here, Fat Face, come you out.' As Fat Face came out his coat was looked at, an' the same button wis off. At this the gardener thought there might be some mistake, so he tried anither and anither, an' aye the same button wis awantin'. At last he turned and bolted out o' the square, wi' twa or three o' his ain crab-yaps rattling about his lugs, an' roars o' laughter frae baith the Govie and the knaps.

"A right good laugh the Govie took, when he saw that it was a trick."

"What guid wid the button hae done him to ken the knap wi'?" asked Toby.

"Oh, at that time a' the buttons used to be brass, and had a stamped picture o' the "Wark" on them, and surely naebody but knaps wid hae them on their claes."

Next morning, Johnstone and Ross waited for Armstrong to see him as he came down from his learning which he looked after in the sixth school. When he appeared they laid their case before him.

"He's a mean, tawnying scadge o' a teller," said Armstrong, after hearing the story. "I'll see some o' the ither lawds about it, an I'll tell you after." Turning on his heel he disappeared under the shadow of the big pillar.

"Skin's in for it this time onyway," said Ross. "If it hadna been for him we widna hae got that pinnin' last nicht."

"Aye, an' had a rare chip-in wi' yon carrots," remarked Johnstone, with a rueful look.

During the afternoon, Armstrong collared Johnstone, telling him to meet him in the lawds' parlour after five o'clock, and to bring his chums with him, and the "kid" that heard Skin tell on them.

"All right," said Johnstone, and passed on.

Meeting Walter and Simpson they had a long walk under the pillars, raking up evidence for the conviction of Skin.

"A tell you what it is," said Walter, "am no gaun to stand it ony longer. He's tawnied ower me jist enough. If he gies me much mair o' it, I'll try him, that's a'."

"He wid be ower much fur you," said Johnstone, with a thoughtful shake of the head. "He's a long way bigger an' aulder than you."

"Am no' carin'," was Walter's plucky rejoinder. "A wis gey near turnin' on him the ither day. Ye ken the lang striped stanes on the outside o' the pend gate? Well, because a widna step them yin at a time jist to please him he gied me a muggin', an' a sair yin to."

"The beast!" was the triple echo.

After tea they got hold of the wee knap and proceeded across the square to the parlours. In a few moments the garr and other five or six lawds came in. Upon hearing how the knaps were caught and the direct evidence given by wee Clerk against Christie they agreed that he should be put out of his schools and greens till after the vacation at least; and as they would be out before the next chance of giving him a snowhouse, they advised Ross to keep it in mind himself and not let the culprit slip.

On getting out to the square again they saw the lawds bullying Skin and giving him his instructions as to future limits. They could see that he took it all with a very bad grace. Edging away, he scowled darkly at his accusers.

CHAPTER IX.

THE Lawds' Examination was approaching. They had got their last suit of new clothes, one distinctive mark being side-pockets and either "Rounders" or "Balmorals." They had tea with Mammie, not forgetting to purloin or pocket a soda-scone in order to "chaw" their less fortunate chums.

After their own examination, which preceded by a week the general one, a half-holiday was given to all. The general examination day I daresay was not so much wished for to exhibit their progress in knowledge and learning, as that it was breaking-up day—the first of a six weeks' scamper to some, and the beginning of an outside life of apprenticeship or further collegiate studies to others. At ten o'clock the gates were opened to the friends of the boys and the public in general. The different class-rooms were taken up by the teachers, and the classes passed through, the boys' friends following them in their progress, and hearing questions put by the examiners and answered by the boys.

The class to which Walter belonged was soon over, and Mrs Crighton, Kate, and Mary were shown through the place. The writing-school was much admired. It was literally covered with specimens—"spacies," as Walter named them,—and drawings of floral designs, vases, heads, mechanical and architectural exhibits, all showing great proficiency in the pen and pencil department of the "Wark" curriculum.

When all the classes were over, the boys assembled in the square. The band took up their stand in front of the pond gate, and played to the marching and counter-marching of the boys, under General Levick. Dinner was then served in the hall, and during the time a table was set in the square in front of the Chapel door. It was filled with prize-books for distribution amongst the successful scholars of the last "half."

On coming out of the hall, the boys hurried away to their wards to secure their bags containing a change of clothing, and other things. Upon re-entering the square, they and their friends congregated round the table, where some of the parlour forms had been put. Although sitting space was not provided for all, sufficient provision was made for some of the older people to rest themselves while witnessing the interesting proceedings. One of the leading Governors took the chair, the other Governors being seated on his right and left.

On rising to present the prizes, the Chairman addressed the boys in a short pithy speech. He gave the usual special instruction and advice to those who were finally leaving the Institution; and also, in name of the Governors, thanked the teachers for the painstaking manner in which it was apparent they had one and all conducted their sections, so as to bring the pupils up to the standard of proficiency which they had witnessed on that occasion.

He then handed the different lads their books, mentioning for what they had been awarded, and calling attention to the fact when any very brilliant "star" was brought forward.

At last, but by no means least, came the presentation of the silver medal.

It was presented to———. The Chairman in handing it over continued: "In presenting this, the highest mark of our appreciation for good conduct and general ability, I may say that we have to-day followed you and listened to you in your section, which is the highest class you can attain in this Institution. My much-respected friend and your Governor on my left, here" (at this remark a very polite bow was made by the Doctor, who had remained standing) "has just been telling me of your-a-most exemplary behaviour and obedience ever since you came into this a-a-a Institution" (hear! hear! and cheers from the boys). "You-a you-a your manners, habits, and conduct have been such as-a as-a could be held up to the others to follow and imitate" (hear! hear! and with loud applause). "So well have you behaved yourself and striven also to-a to-a rise as you have done in your various studies and-a and-a have succeeded-a-have succeeded in gaining this special award, it is a great pleasure to us, and very gratifying indeed, when we find that you are-a-a not to forsake the pursuit of scientific instruction, but are still to be under the care of the Governors of George Heriot's Hospital as a Bursar at the College of this City. We would advise you to carry on there the good intents and exemplary integrity which-a-you have-a-taken as your line of conduct here, and we have no doubt that future years will see you rise to eminence and-a-a prosperity. I have great pleasure, sir, in presenting you with this medal."

The lad made a bow, and amidst great applause received from the hand of the Chairman a morocco case containing the silver medal.

A few remarks by the Doctor, followed, principally regarding the time for returning—the 20th day of September. He particularly requested the boys not to get into harm's way. This wound up the proceedings, and in a short time the "Wark" was deserted. A few, indeed, had to remain in owing to their parents living at too great a distance, or perhaps not being either prepared with accommodation, or unable to take their boys home. Some went out for the first fortnight, some for the last; others a week or two in the middle of the holiday, or just as their parents desired. One or two had to stay in the "Wark" the whole six weeks.

For several reasons, Walter was among those who had only asked for the last two weeks. One reason was that if he had to be at home for any length of time Mrs Crighton, owing to her scanty room, would have to part with one of her boarders, which she could ill afford to do. Another reason was that as his mother lived so near he could easily run home on the two days, Wednesday and Saturday, on which they got out. Then, of course, the boys were not taxed with lessons as they were when the school was "up," so that Walter was readily reconciled to stay in till the last fortnight. His mother had arranged with an aunt of her own in Dunfermline to take him for that time, and Walter was as delighted as the rest were.

On the night following the afternoon of the examination he made his way up to the "Wark," not without certain qualms, reasoning with himself that, on the whole, it was not quite fair that he should thus have to turn in. However, he knew it could not be helped, and then to-morrow was a holiday. This last thought made things look a little brighter, and turning into the gate he made his way up.

On getting into the square he found a number of his fellow unfortunates, if we may so call them, gathered together. By good luck, Ross was to be in three of the weeks. He had, however, not arrived yet. Walter accordingly took a survey of his companions. Three or four lawds, not a day old yet, but very important looking, half-a-dozen cholds, and about a dozen knaps and kids — these made up the lot, between twenty and thirty in all.

"Hullo, Crighton! how long are you out for"? said one.

"The last fortnight," replied Walter. Some smiled, others shrugged their shoulders, and a few remarked: "You're no' sae bad as me; a'm out nane o' the time."

Ross had now come in, and presently he was consoling Walter with some account of his experiences of last year when he had been out just the same time. "Mun it's rare to be in on the vacance, although a widna like to be in athegither. A lot depends on what maister is on duty: some never bother you, others are gey strict. But ye'll find it's the best o' fun naething to dae, an' ony amount o' liberty. Come on an' we'll see if the first eleven's left out their bats and stumps." When he had looked behind the 'cond school door, Ross performed a small "break down."

"Oh, jimity," he exclaimed, "they've no only left the bats an' stumps, but a pair o' auld pads and a right hand wicket glove. Hold on a minute; let's see if ony o' the lawds are in the first eleven."

Looking round the corner, he said, "There's Cowan, Hunter, Jeffrey, and Hislop. No, there's no' yin o' them, as far as I can see. It's a' richt, we'll hae a rare time o't."

"But we haven't a ball," said Walter.

"Never mind that," replied Ross, "A ken where there's a rare solid yin in the lodge, that Magnus took frae a knap fur playing wi' it in the learning. I'll cadge it off him; a ken he'll gie's it; he's no' a bad sort."

Sauntering out into the square, instructions were being given as to what wards they were to occupy, namely, the fifth and sixth. Ross nudging Walter, whispered, "That's good, the best wee wards for the vacance, no' ower big; an' then Ja-ra-pa sleeps there, and he's quiet enough. After a short service of prayer in the seventh school, the boys went up to the ward, which was just above in the same stair.

Says Ross, "This is the ward we'll be shifted to when we come in, only it will be the wee ward. There are only twelve beds in it, but it's a cheery yin." On going in, the first compartment was the wash-house with its rows of basins, towels, and small mirrors. On the right was a door which led to the "wee," and on the left one leading to the big ward. Even the big ward was small, its largeness being only comparative. These wards were, in fact, the two smallest in the house.

After their beds had all been pointed out to them, Walter and Ross managed to get their's so that they could draw them close, and have a rare chat at nights. Cowan, "Puggie" Cowan, as he was called, was nominated monitor. He was a very nice, kindly fellow, rather small and sharp in the features, with a slight burr in his speech. Ross was sure he would make a good monitor as there "wisna ony o' the tawnie in him." The wee ward was to be kept in subjection by "Duggie" Hislop, and as there were only two or three small boys in it, his duties would not be very onerous. So far as the ward was concerned things went on much as usual, only a certain amount of extra liberty was allowed, or rather little faults were passed unchecked.

Next day was apparently enjoyed by all, and they returned at night in better spirits. In the morning the bell was rung for rising at eight o'clock, and breakfast came at nine, as usual, after a short service in the seventh school room. At ten o'clock all had to make an appearance in the parlour where the teacher on duty gave them an hour's lessons in a very general way, often reading to them an instructive tale. A very pleasant hour, rather than otherwise, it always was.

When the master had left at eleven, Ross gave Crighton a slap on the shoulder.

"Well now, Wattie, what do you say? We are clear till bedtime; we've only to take our dinner, and "chit and milk." What do you say? What has it to be?"

"I don't know," said Walter; "it's ower hot for cricket."

"Come on then, an' we'll hae a turn right round the greens," said Ross; and arm in arm the pair passed round under the pillars and out at the pend gate.

It was a splendid day for a quiet stroll round the green grass banks which surrounded the "Wark." As they came out on to the balustrades, both as if by mutual agreement stopped and had a good look around. Arm in arm they stood at the top of the 'ird green stairs and gazed with delight on the scene before them. The bright warm

sun, which had not yet that oppressive feeling that is always
felt towards mid-day in the July and August months,
gilded everything with its golden rays. There, in front,
was the beautiful lawn. On the 'ird greens were a patch of
knaps, some with their coats cast, setting the wickets for
a lazy game. Others were lying on their backs, trying, one
would fancy, to penetrate the bright shining orb above.
Then there was the grand old plantation of trees and shrubs
skirting the green all round, conspicuous amongst which was
the rhododendron in full bloom, overshadowed by numerous
sprays of bright apple blossom, which alas! never came to
fruit for the knap. At short intervals there were the large
laburnum trees, rich in their wealth of bright golden
blossom, and even the humble pansy could be clearly seen
clustering round the verges. The grand old castle stood out
boldly in the back-ground, showing the high window of
the room where the unfortunate Queen Mary Stuart lived,
and from whose dizzy heights she swung her infant son in
safety to the rocks below. There was the half-moon battery
with its tall tapering flagstaff, from which fluttered the
Royal Scottish Standard, and the huge brazier, where in
times of trouble the beacon fire was kindled to warn the
lieges of coming danger.

Still further towards the right, the eye followed the wall
of the castle approach. its shapely little ornamental turrets
adding a charm to what was only a simple "dyke." Then
came into view the high and beautifully proportioned spire
of the Tolbooth Church, on the clock of which the eager
knap could catch the "five, ten, fifteen to hour." Following round still further, you espied the crown-like steeple
of St Giles, with its long arching arms grasping, as it

were, the sweet chiming bells which we loved to listen to as the afternoon came round. Then last, but not least, there was the Heriotties' place of worship—the place where many generations of garriers gone before had worshipped: the old Greyfriars Church, with its plain, but still ecclesiastical, look, only relieved by the heavy buttresses which surround it. This can only convey but a very poor idea of the beautiful view obtained by our young friends on that delightful morning.

Making their way down, they crossed the green, and turning under the bank, wandered round, chatting about what they were to be doing, both indoors and outdoors on the days of leave.

"You ken we're gawn to get an excursion to Roslin in about a fortnight," said Ross. "We aye get that when we are in on the vacance, either to there, or somewhere no' very far away. They say that it is often a long way better than the knaps' excursion, but as I have telt you before, it depends on the maister on duty; if he's a guid yin, then it's a' right, if he's a birsy soul, then it's a' wrang."

"I hope it's Cockie," said Walter.

"Same here," agreed Ross.

Several projects were made, plots hatched, and old stories told, which put past the time until the dinner bell rang.

In the afternoon a side was got up at cricket, and when that was done, there was a game at "big shovie," at the bottom of the 'ird green stairs. Ross being rather an adept with his "doliker," he very nearly "rouxed" the lot. After "chit and milk," there was another game, perhaps at tip and run, or a left-handed side at the stumps was finished up with a smart turn at "swipie." This closed the day. In such a manner every day was got over very pleasantly during the holidays.

In a few days a large staff of workmen—painters, plumbers, joiners, and others—had brought their tools and materials, ladders and scaffolding. Apparently there were great alterations and renovations in contemplation.

As time went on, the day for the little trip arrived. The boys were taken by vans to Roslin, and on arriving they were marched down to the dell where they had a very enjoyable time. During the day, races and games of various kinds were indulged in for prizes given by those in charge. Two or three of the Governors having come along with them, the knaps managed to draw upon their pockets.

One of the great events was a race which arose out of an argument between the Doctor and Cockie about the judging of one of the handicaps. It was agreed that they, accompanied by two of the Governors, should run a race. This set the knaps fairly jumping with delight. Just fancy, F. W. Bedford, LL.D., stretching across the grass at racing speed! After a good deal of laughter on their own part, the four were at last got into line.

The Doctor, taking his hat off and passing his fingers once or twice through his long black hair, stood right foot foremost awaiting the signal from Shinnie, who was holding the handkerchief. Cockie was rubbing his fingers and thumbs, and projecting the tip of his tongue at a rapid rate from between his lips, swaying backwards and forwards in a manner peculiar to himself. The other two waited in their own particular styles, all the attitudes being certainly far from professional.

"Go," cried Shinnie, at the same time dropping the handkerchief.

Away set the competitors. They kept very well abreast for a minute or two, but the Doctor with his enormous strides soon took the lead. On turning the post and coming down the "straight," they were seen at their best. On they came like four wind-mills on the loose. Unfortunately, just as they were homing in grand style, an uneven part of the ground or something else caught Cockie's foot, and over he pitched to the delight of the knaps. No harm was done by the fall, as he could not have touched the winner, and there was no second place prize.

As one of the boys was poking into the holes and corners about the dell in search of nests, he came upon a nest of young bats. These he brought out to daylight, and exhibited in great triumph to his chums. Levick allowed the lads to "roll their hoop" as far as was good for them with the little animals; after which he made them put the tiny things back into their nest. Having visited the Chapel, where they saw the 'prentice pillar, and other sights about the place, all returned home highly pleased with the day's outing.

One night after retiring to rest some of the knaps were awakened by a terrible noise, just as if the steeple were tumbling down upon them. The cause of the unexpected rousing soon became evident, for a vivid flash of lightning lit up the ward as bright as day. It turned out to be, indeed, a terrible storm. Flash succeeded flash in rapid succession, accompanied by loud, cannon-like thunder peals. It began about twelve o'clock, and raged for over an hour-and-a-half. People living in a city understand how terror-striking is a midnight storm; but I feel sure that when one of those tearing cracks broke over the "Wark" quadrangle it made the juveniles quake in a way unknown to their elders.

Right thankful were Walter and his friends as the sounds became more distant and less frequent. Several stories of former storms were told, one of the knaps stating as a fact that on one occasion he had laid a handful of pen nibs on the balusters, and that the lightning flash came down and scattered them in all directions. One little fellow sat up in his bed, and, when quietness had been secured, he began: "Long ago there used to be kept in the 'Wark' a big dug."

At this a groan of horror ran round the ward. Everyone buried his head in the blankets. Whether he ever finished his tale or not it is impossible to say, for very soon they were all asleep.

Next day was bright and warm; the storm of the previous night had cleared away a dulness which had been hanging about for some time. The greens were not long in drying and were soon in good condition for an enjoyable side. Throwing up the bat between Cowan and Hislop, "A flat or a round for the innin's" was the query.

Cowan cried a round: it was a flat, so Hislop had it.

"I'll take Smith," said Hislop.

"I'll take Clerk," said his opponent; and so on till all present had been chosen.

"I suppose baith sides field," said Captain Hislop, his side having got first innings.

"All right" was the response, and at it they went.

"You take wickets, Clerk, and I'll bowl wi' Wight, six an' over."

The fields being spread, play began, and at length resulted in a victory for Cowan's team by 39 runs.

Being warm and heated with their exertions, Cowan remarked to Ross: "Man, I could take a bathe fine the now."

After a little consideration Ross replied, "I'll tell you where we could get yin."

"Where?" queried Cowan, stopping short in the moping of the sweat from his neck with his handkerchief.

"Maybe Clerk will come. Cry him ower and see what he says," added Ross. Cowan beckoned to Clerk, who came, running.

"Ross says he kens where we can get a dook; will you gang?"

"I ken mysel'," said Clerk—"Portie."

"No quite sae far as that," said Ross; "but it's a kind o' a secret, and if yer no gaun, am no gaun to tell you where it is."

"Well, if it's no' far, I'll gang," said Clerk.

"Come on then," said Ross, and leading the way straight across the greens he laid himself down on the top of the bank—Cowan, Clerk, and Walter sitting down beside him.

"Well, what's the next move?" asked the captain.

"Take yer time; gie a look and see if you see *Sel'* about."

Sel' not being observed, Ross quietly rolled over the top of the bank into the shrubbery, calling to the others to "smool" down as quietly as possible. This was done, and bolting down through the bushes and across the walk, Cowan nearly broke his neck falling over an iron seat immediately in front of a bush he passed through. On reaching the bottom, they found themselves at the wall of the Heriot Bridge Day School with its trellised windows.

"Up this way," said Ross; and they turned towards the west end of the building. On reaching the point where the dyke joins the school they stopped, Ross holding up his leg.

"Gie's a hist up," he said.

Cowan, catching hold of his foot, sent him up to the top of the wall, where, after getting a hold, he soon scrambled up altogether. All were quickly on the top and sitting astride the dyke. On the other side there was a small court with one or two out-houses. Crawling over the tiles of one of the latter Ross opened a small door, and there inside was the bath.

"How did you find it out?" asked Cowan.

"Oh, I was ower last vacance, although I wasna in it, but we'll better strip," and suiting the action to the word, he cast off his jacket and vest. The rest following suit, all were soon in a state of nature, their clothes lying on the slates. The cistern in front of them was the one which supplied the school! It was a large one, having more the appearance of a bath than anything else, and on such a warm day the water looked delightfully cool.

Ross as leader popped in first. In depth it took him up to the waist.

"How does it feel?" asked Clerk.

"F—F—Fine," he stammered. "St—St—Stunning."

On this the rest followed, and were soon floundering in the drinking-water.

"By gum! this is a cauld bath," said Cowan, and his feet slipping in the slime on the bottom, down he went over the head. This was enough for him. Out he went with a jump, and squatting down on the tiles rubbed himself vigorously with his handkerchief and shirt. The others taking it more quietly, enjoyed a good though extremely cold bath. Drying themselves in the same way as Cowan, all were soon ready, and, closing the door, they scrambled back and joined their companions in the greens.

CHAPTER X.

THE holiday time soon went past. Walter had been to Dunfermline, and enjoyed his outing in the country immensely, as only a knap could, freed from all the customary restraint. At last the night fixed for his return to the "Wark" arrived, and with heavy heart and a lump in his throat, Walter, accompanied by his mother and sisters, trudged away up to Lauriston, where he was soon swallowed up by the grim gateway — a woe-begone little figure with all his troubles before him. He took his bag up to his ward, and then joined the crowd of knaps in the square. Almost all were in groups of six or seven, arm in arm, quietly walking round, recounting their various adventures and pleasures, some actually dropping a silent tear in quiet corners, wondering how they should sleep in the "Wark" after such a revival of home experiences.

On the bell ringing for "fall in," all turned into their places, and the doors of the Chapel were thrown open. Two deep, right face, and forward they went into the well-known place of worship. All had been moved up a form or two. The new lawds, as yet hardly realising their important position, were looking about them and smiling at their chums. Really they could not help it. The consciousness that one had become a lawd in the "Wark" was about equal to the feeling of being raised to the peerage in civil life. When all were seated, the few minutes' wait for the Doctor was spent in gazing round the old place to see if any alterations had been made on it. No alterations could be seen. It was in a certain sense refreshing to look above the door and read the familiar words—*Gloria in excelsis Deo*, and to see the white aprons of the "wifies" peeping through the carved balusters at each end. Presently there was heard the soft, swift step of the Doctor, as he entered in full sail, smiling a welcome back to the boys at both sides on the way up to the pulpit. A psalm was sung to that well known tune, "Evan," which always kept its place, both for its simplicity and its beauty. A passage from the big black Bible, and a fervent prayer to the Almighty for the preservation of his boys from harm and malicious conduct put, as it were, the cap on for another term of the old régime.

On the Doctor coming downstairs, the new lists of the different wards were read out, Walter being shifted as Ross had said to the sixth. The two boys had a narrow escape of being separated, Ross being the eldest and Walter the youngest in it. It was one comfort that they were still to be together.

Going upstairs they found that they had several new companions. There were only twelve altogether, but some very nice, jolly little fellows. All were well enough known to Walter, but being in the same ward always raised new associations. One of the cholds was monitor, not one of the tawnying sort, who always cadged for crockles and gave you a muggin' because they were scrimped. Perhaps, reader, if you be not fortunate enough to be an auld callant, the explanation of a "crockle scrimped o' the cawrie" will not be out of place. Firstly, we must anatomise a "dose." A "dose" was literally a small loaf, the different portions being a round crockle or top crust, a flat crockle or bottom crust, and the cawrie the soft bread between. Then again there was a variety called a "fan," and another a double fan. The first was one of the outside of the batch, having the crust on the side as well as the top and bottom; and the second had the crust on the top, bottom, side and end.

Now, when anyone was "awn a crockle," perhaps in part payment of some debt, or for some favour received or in promise, or it might be to court the good countenance of some one in greater power, it was expected that that crockle would be pulled off without the cawrie which adhered to it being trimmed off by the giver. Some possibly hungry knap would, however, before delivering it up, have it so thin and light that you might blow it past the first millar easily enough. That was a "scrimp crockle." There were some, not many, of these crockle cadgers, and monitors always had a great deal of opportunity to cadge if they wished.

After a good night's rest and breakfast, the next thing was the re-arrangement of classes or sections. Walter got a shift into a class which gave him a deal more to do, and robbed him of some of his old play-hours. He would now have penmanship other than "whips" and "strokes," and several other extras which he did not have before. One feature which in a day or two made a little novelty, was the arrival of another batch of "new-come-in-yins." By this time Walter was up past the hall door in his position in the square and thoroughly initiated, quite able to teach any little unfortunate to whom he took a fancy. There was, however, a custom which unfortunately Walter had not known, namely, that of the "Birthday Bush." His birthday coming in September, he mentioned it to someone, who did for him by telling the bigger knaps. The latter coaxing Walter down to the greens collared him by the neck and heels, carried him to the cradle or Geordie's bush, and with a "one, two, three," landed him right in the middle of it. Being a prickly holly bush, trimmed in the shape of a small couch, the getting out of it was as painful an affair as the being pitched in, but, as it was a custom, Walter took it all in good part. Of course, he would have it out on some other one before his own time was done.

"LEVICK."*

One very pleasant addition to Walter's course of instruction was the weekly class for military drill. Everyone liked Levick's mornings, when drill was substituted for preparation, a different class being taken each morning. Not only was the open-air exercise enjoyed, but Levick himself was a warm friend and favourite of the knaps. He combined with the office of Gate-Keeper and Wardsman, the dignified posts of

---

* The sword here shown was presented to him by the "London Auld Callants Club."

Drill Instructor and Bandmaster. He was a fine sample of the old soldier, tall, straight as a rash, and with a most dignified bearing. He had seen a good deal of the world, and enjoyed spinning most marvellous yarns to the knaps when he was, as he phrased it, "out of harness"—that is, when he was gate-keeper. His camaraderie with the knaps on these occasions was only equalled by his assumption of gravity, dignity, and decorum when "in harness," that is, when he was the drill instructor or the bandmaster, and then he enlarged on the heinousness of "insubordination, the greatest crime in the army."

If anyone knew how to humour, amuse, and instruct, morally and physically, it was Levick. Punctually at seven o'clock, there he was with his cane under his arm quietly waiting until the boys had gathered on the gravel, generally on the east side of the house, in front of the kids' parlour windows. That was for company drill: battalion drill on the Saturday mornings was always in the square. The first salutation generally was, "Come now, boys, fall into line." The knaps would rush to their places. "Number off:" "One," "two," "three," "four," and so on, hardly a boy speaking in his natural voice.

"Even numbers stand fast; odd numbers one pace to the rear and one to the right." Commencing with the first syllable, one, two, this brought the boys two deep.

"Right hand man, stand fast; remainder, mark time; close up to the right; march."

All having closed up, "Halt, steady, eyes front."

"Here, you boy, don't you know your right from your left?" Here he walked with a slow steady step to the left of the company, and glancing along the line, shouted "Dress up a little in the centre. Not so much there, you, Fraser; don't you know what a little means?"

Good old soul! it is a wonder he kept his temper at all. Very likely Fraser would be about half a yard in front of everybody else, just to provoke him. Walking again to the front of the line, and on turning round some one was sure to be out of position, or after some nonsense.

"ATTENTION!"

"Steady there, I tell you; I think you boys imagine I come here only to play with you. Now I don't mind playing with you as much as you like when not at drill; when you are here you're in harness and so am I; steady! When I am at the gate, I am gate-keeper, but when I'm here, I'm your master."

At this point one of the front rank caps flew out on to the middle of the gravel.

"I say there, you, Sharp, I'll cut you as short as a carrot; pick up that cap."

This order was given to the owner of the cap, who was standing as square as possible, with his little fingers to the seams of his trousers, and looking very innocent.

"Some of you boys come here to this Hospital and think you have nothing to do but eat, play, and sleep, and learn to be gentlemen; but that won't pull you through the world; you will find that out when it is too late. But it is just like throwing water over a duck my telling you this. If you had been brought up where I was, where we had to travel miles to school, with nothing but a bit of tartan round our hurdies, and had to carry some meal with us for our dinner, which was put into a hole in the rock along with rain water and a flat stone laid over it until we came out of school—that was our food."

"Where did you carry the meal?" queried one little fellow.

"Oh, you had to carry it in your trousers pocket," said Levick.

"I thought you said you had naething but a bit tartan round you," said another, at which all had a good laugh, Levick himself included. He could enjoy a joke as well as anybody.

"And did you get nothing else but the meal and water?" asked another.

"Only a good thrashing across the *brans* of my legs with a bunch of heather, to make my legs strong," was the answer; and walking along the back of the line he would give practical demonstration in a small way with his cane.

"Come now, 'tention! belly in, breast out, head well elevated; prepare for extension motions: right hand man, stand fast; remainder, mark time; two paces to the left, march! halt! right-about-face; number off again."

They numbered off. "Front rank—odd numbers, nine paces, even numbers, six paces; rear rank—odd numbers, three paces, even numbers, stand fast — march." This brought the company into a position in which they had full freedom to use their arms without interfering with each other.

"Right about face.—The first extension motion.—At the word 'one,' bring the hands into a line with the chin; 'two,' put them as far back as possible." This was gone on with and continued until all were red in the face.

"Second extension motion.—At the word 'one,' bring the hands in the same position as in the first motion, with the fingers closed. At the word 'two,' put them straight in a line with the shoulders. At the word 'three,' swing them backwards and forwards in a circle until the word 'halt' is given."

"Now then! one, two, three." At this, all arms were swinging merrily.

"Halt! Here I say, you, Farquhar, don't you know the difference between forwards and backwards and backwards and forwards?"

Walking up to him, he took the boy's hands. He was a tall, raw-looking boy. He was carefully shown the way and again Levick stepped out to the front of the line.

"Attention! one, two, three;" and all were again on the swing, everyone the right way but Farquhar, who kept swinging his arms in the opposite direction, to the infinite amusement of the rest of the now breathless boys, and the great annoyance of Levick.

"Halt! Halt! Halt! here you chuckle-headed fellow; surely your mother keeps a mangle, and has had you turning it for her."

This was a great piece of fun for the boys, who forthwith baptised the lad "Chuckle," a name which he religiously received ever after. The rest of the motions and the bayonet exercise were gone through; then all into line and break off, and the hour was finished.

During the afternoon, as Ross and Walter were coming out of the pend gate, they met a young lad known to the knaps as "Jock." whose duty it was to wind up the "Wark" clock every week.

"Come on," he said. Having the key of the belfry door up they went through the writing-school. On opening the first door, they entered a little square room lined round with presses, having trellis doors, behind which the brass instruments belonging to the band were shining. In the corner lay the big drum and its two little friends, the kettle drums, quietly resting near with their buffs up. Another door led into the tower. Opposite was a ladder-looking stair up which they mounted. On reaching the top, they found themselves in a large barn-looking room in which was kept a quantity of lumber. For example, there were the properties, the crown, and other emblems used in the June Day decorations, all shorn of their glory, and with a look about them as if they had lain in the same position for ages.

In one corner stood a pole, perched on the top of which was a gilt cock; it had evidently been used for carrying on some of the processional occasions in connection with the "Wark." Sundry other articles of a like character lay about.

Up another stair, and there they were beside the huge bell which tolled the hours of pleasure and of pain, pleasant enough to hear when it meant "fall in" on a Saturday morning; painful enough when it heralded the hour for a class with a birsy master for whom you were unprepared. In the centre was the machinery of the clock, with its many wheels, more like those of some intricate engine than the works of a clock. There was a deep pit-like box which went down to the writing-school flat, where swung the heavy pendulum and great weights which Jock was labouring with a crank handle to raise, so as to give it another week's life. With the help of the boys, this was soon done, and at their request Jock took them up a ladder into a roomy loop-holed turret chamber, and opening a door they now got out on to the ledge or steeple barty running round the tower, as near the "Wark" weather-cock as they possibly could get in a legitimate way. Here a splendid view of the town and and the country for many miles around was obtained. It was rather a dizzy height, however, and the boys soon retraced their steps.

Next morning, as Walter and one or two of his chums were "larking" in the connie, playing round the big pillar, Skin passed, and putting out his foot, over went Walter, sprawling under the kids' parlour window.

Skin passed on, Walter meanwhile gathering himself together and feeling very bitter towards his old enemy. One or two of his chums clustered round to sympathise with Walter. They were all strong in their condemnation of Skin's eternal tawnying.

"I've a good mind to try him," said Walter.

"So have I," said another.

"An' me too," said a third.

These remarks had not long been uttered when they were carried to Skin by some one cadging for favour; for as Skin was beginning to be a general terror to the smaller knaps, his friendship was a good deal sought after by some. In a short time he came along from the parlours with two or three of his friends.

"Did you say you'd try me, Crighton?" he asked. "And you, and you, and you?" he added, pointing to the others who had spoken.

No one answered, all seeming to slink away from his brutal rage.

"Gie them a' a muggin," was the suggestion of one of his chums. The suggestion was put into effect.

They were pulled into the place of punishment not far distant, and each had a "muggin'." Walter was crying bitterly, not so much from the pain of the blows, as from a feeling of passion at the bully. One of the cholds, named Fairbairn, coming in and seeing the youths crying and others sympathising, inquired what was wrong.

On being told, Fairbairn turned to Walter with the query—

"Did you say that, Crighton?"

"Yes," answered Walter.

"An' will you try him?"

"Yes," he replied, this time in a very decided manner.

"A' richt, I'll see fair play."

By this time a good number had gathered round. Away went Fairbairn to search for Skin. When Skin came he was to all appearance bristling with rage.

"Where will we gang?" he asked Fairbairn.

"Up to the sixth school," was the answer. Up the stair went the crowd, numbering by this time about twenty or so knaps, big and little. The sixth school was on the first flat of the north-east wing; it had plenty of floor room for any encounter of this kind.

It was entered by a little dark lobby, from which doors opened into the seventh school, a lavatory for the use of the warders, and the fourth ward.

"BAT" IN THE SIXTH SCHOOL.

All were in and the door was shut. Some got on to the desk, others on to the master's platform; some perched themselves on the window-sills, and the rest sat on the forms. Fairbairn and some of the lawds acting as backers, bottle-holders, &c., were thinking it rather a good joke to see a knap just past the hall door trying a chold a good bit past "mammie's connie." They never expected but that Crighton would be half-killed, and were prepared to stop the fight before it went too far.

Fairbairn stepping up to Walter helped him off with his jacket, at the same time whispering to him, "He canna bat at a'; dinna be fud for him, and when you hit him, strike richt atween the een." Walter was not a bit afraid even when he saw the big hulk squaring madly at him.

After a bit of sparring, the first round passed without much damage on either side. It had, in fact, only the effect of showing Walter that Skin was not so very much to be afraid of, notwithstanding that he *was* big. In the second round, a hit from his antagonist sent Walter reeling over like a nine-pin, but the blow being on his shoulder, it did not do him much harm. On facing up for the third round, Walter, without giving Skin much time for "bantin jumping," struck exactly where Fairbairn had told him, "richt atween the een," and at a moment when Skin was lowering his head for a rush. That upper cut was a lucky one for Walter.

The bully never raised his "nugget" again, but grasping his arms round it, ran to the wall, Crighton following him pommelling him right and left, up and down, until he had completely taken satisfaction out of him. Walter actually stopped for want of breath, amid the shouts of joy from his chums, and a good clap on the back from Fairbairn.

"Good lad, sound pluck; that's it, Crighton, that'll cook his goose for him," he said.

On raising his head, Skin's face was hardly recognisable. His left eye was swollen underneath, almost like an egg. That blow had just happened to land on the right place, otherwise it might have fared differently with our little friend. As it was, all were glad; it would put an end to Skin's tricks, for he had "gien in," and that was what was wanted. Skin got a few more challenges, but all were quietly refused. Walter felt really sorry when he looked at the fellow's face, and wondered how he could have had the strength to do it.

All that day Skin slunk within the parlours, with his handkerchief at his cheek, "maukin" with the toothache. Walter's friends were in high glee over this event; in fact it was not only a victory for Walter, but it ensured peace from a fiend for all the younger knaps and kids.

That day passed over all right, and the next being Saturday, they had assembled in the square as usual before going out. As was his custom, the Doctor came into the square, and beginning at the eldest, walked slowly along the line, taking a glance at each one, just to see that they were in order to appear before the outside world. On coming to Skin, who was standing with his head turned so as to escape the Doctor's glance, he stopped, and putting his hands behind his back, looked hard at him without saying anything. After staring for some time, he said quietly, "Turn your head this way, Christie." Skin, his eyes on the ground, turned his face round.

"Step out here," said the Doctor.

Skin stepped out, never daring to raise his eyes. Another wait for about a minute or so, and the question was slowly asked—"Who did it?" Skin would not answer; whether it was that he did not want to tell, or that he was ashamed to say, he knew best himself.

Again the query was put in the same measured manner.

"Crighton did it," said Skin, in a low voice.

"Crighton!" said the Doctor, opening his eyes very wide, and glancing down the line until they rested upon poor Walter, who felt inclined to shrink into his boots. There is no doubt that the worthy Doctor knew the character of Christie as well as the boys did, although he never had any good grounds to interfere.

"Crighton," he called, "come here, my boy."

Walter walked slowly across the square and stood before his enemy and the Doctor, feeling like a condemned culprit.

"Did you do this to Christie's face?" was the question.

"Yes, sir," said Walter.

"Tell me how," asked the Governor, in a kindly manner.

"I said I would fight him, and I did it, sir," said Walter.

After another pause the Doctor, remarked: "I really cannot see how a little fellow like you could make such a mark on a boy's face, and he nearly twice your size, but I have a good idea how it has all been. You cannot leave the Hospital to-day," he said, turning to Skin: "and you, Crighton, will be confined for two hours just to show you how I disapprove of all such conduct."

The boys were then marched out, and the two left to console each other as best they could. Ross promised to call in and tell Walter's mother why he was confined.

The two hours were not long in going past, and Walter was soon at home, receiving a severe lecture from his mother for getting into such a scrape. After hearing all the outs and ins of the affair Mrs Crighton was less severe; indeed, Walter had often, with tears in his eyes, complained to his mother about the usage he got from Christie.

When Walter went in at night Mrs Crighton gave him a small packet of sock to give to his adversary, as in her heart she really felt for the boy who had been kept from getting home, all through her son. The little present was faithfully delivered to Skin by a knap, though he never knew from whom it came.

One of Walter's new classes was advanced writing. He had passed "whips" and "strokes," and was spluttering in full text, such words as "Zimmerman" and "Grammarian," &c. As Fuflie, the writing teacher, was rather a good master, the knaps always got on very well with him. He had a pair of tawse of thick, heavy leather, with two tails, more frightful to look at than painful to feel. The worst of this instrument of punishment was that when a knap was affecting to be very intent on his copy and taking great pains (the desks and seats being low), and he would be, as it was termed, "trying hard and sticking out," he would get an upward stroke, not so sore as it was startling, accompanied with the question, "Is that the way to hold your pen?" or, "Sit up right on your seat," "Look alive and get a five" (five being his maximum), or some such remark. It made the knap feel very angry, and he was almost certain to blurt out something punishable, for which perhaps one or two were given and taken just as a matter of course.

Fuflie had rather a metrical turn, which very much amused the boys. Sometimes he would come out with long strings of rhyme, such as—

"Hay, come up this way, and I'll give you something to say; you've been at it all day; you come here to work and not to play; come along, sir, and I'll make you bray."

"Moyes, is it you that's making all that noise, disturbing all the boys with your little ploys? I'll be at you in a troise.

"Short, I see you at your sport, I'll be at you for't, and give you something that will make you snort."

"Hutton, you apparently don't give a button: that capital's just like a leg of mutton."

"Baillie, you come here daily: your time you shilly-shally; you can't write a page but it looks so scaly; come up sir, till I give you a touch of the taillie."

"Wright, I'm sure that page is such a fright, what do you say? It's bad light? I rather think you've bad sight; come up here and you'll get something tight, with all my might, to try and put you right."

"Grant, I'm sure you have a want; why do you make your downstrokes so scant? Make them thicker and a little more to the slant, attend to that now, or I'll give you something that will make you pant."

"Ramage, come up for damage."

These and countless other rhymes were generally accompanied with two or three stripes, mostly pretty "milky." A good deal of eye-wetting and fulling had to be done to make him think he was hurting. It was rather a nice room, the writing-school, with its clean white-washed walls, two rows of double desks running up the middle; flaps here and there formed lockers which the older boys claimed in rotation; and, as these desks had keys, they were very convenient. Along the centre were rows of bottles which supplied both sides with ink, seldom in good condition. As likely as not some tricky lad had put a pinch of sherbet into each, which made the ink rise about twice as high as the bottle, so that they were more like a row of black sponges lying along the desk than anything else.

The English teacher was the "wee Dig." He was not a bad fellow, but he knew tolerably well how to raise and drop his leather. One of his methods for grinding his scholars up in their geography was to make one boy question another. One asked the other to point out as quickly as he possibly could, a country, town, river, &c., upon the map. On this particular day the map of Europe was hanging up, and the game was going on (for it was rather a game than anything else) when one of the boys in a hurried manner cried out "Greece" to Wilson. The master looked at the little fellow, and asked, "What did you say? Greasy Wilson?"

At this a hearty laugh was taken, and of course from that day the youth was known only as "Greasy Wilson."

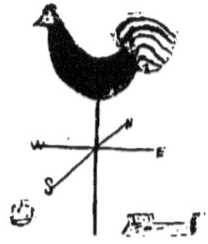

CHAPTER XI.

ONE night, when they were leaving Chapel and going up to the ward, Ross took Walter by the arm and asked him whether he would make one of a party who were going (as he put it) "ower to the auld wife's to roox her pear tree." "It's rare fun," he added; "she keeps a pig, and if we dinna get mony pears we'll hae a thump at the pig."

Walter had a good idea where the auld wife's was, as the direction had often been pointed out to him in his walks along the 'ird green banks, and he longed to have a look at the grumphie.

" Well, when are you gaun ?" he asked.

"Oh, the morn's nicht, about half-an-hour after the hall at tea time."

" Whae else is gaun ?" asked Walter.

" It was Johnstone that asked me," said Ross, " and he says that Sinclair and Fowler's coming and maybe Kidd, but he's awfu' fur bursting out laughing, and micht spoil the fun, so they'll likely no let him gang. However, we'll see."

At this moment they heard a yelping and barking outside.

" What's that ?" asked Ross ; " it's like a dug."

Going over to the pend gate, which was shut and locked, they listened.

"A ken what it is," said Walter, "it's a wee terrier that I've seen auld Peter, the gardener, chasing about fur this day or twa; whenever it's put out it aye wants in again. He put it into the Vennel twice yesterday, but as soon as the wicket's opened, it just bolts in again. It's an ill-natured little beggar. I was gaun tae clap it the ither day when it turned round and showed its teeth—just like yin o' yon monkeys in the menagerie, when we gien them the nit-shells fu' o' soap and cayenne pepper." They chuckled quietly to themselves at the reminiscence, and made their way up to the ward.

After they had been some time in bed and the gas lowered, and very probably all in the wee ward asleep, the door was quietly opened, and in popped the black pate of one of the fifth ward boys. He glanced round and then returned to his own apartment. One of the younger knaps was made to "cleek for *sel*" on the top of the stair, and he with a very bad grace drew on his socks and sneaked out to the stair landing. Crouching down by the pillar which ran up the centre (they were all wheel stairs) he listened for the approach of the wardsman.

After he had been fixed, the knap who had looked into the wee ward marshalled his forces, and the lot of eleven white-chalkered warriors were in line, each carrying his pillow over his shoulder. As one of the twelve in Walter's ward was in the sick-room with spine disease (from which he never fully recovered), only eleven were prepared for the sortie.

At the signal, the miller and his men crossed the washing-house, and opening the door quietly stationed themselves at a bed apiece. "One, two, three," and as many times down came the eleven "bowsters" on as many heads before the suddenly-awakened knaps could realise who was knocking at their dream-gates. Ross' bed was the one against which the ward door opened, and he, knowing the game, jumped up, and with a push shut it before the party had time to withdraw. Seizing hold of his own "bowster," he called to his chums to do the same.

Everyone responded and soon there was a fine shindy; Ross being a pretty strongly-built lad, and well up to twirling the feathers, kept them well back from the only egress from the room. No quarter was asked or given, and in a short time each pillow was more like an Indian club than anything else—a wonderful weapon at anyrate, when properly wielded. If any of the novices missed giving his stroke, he had his own weapon, lock, stock, and barrel, round his neck like a cravat, and, before he could extricate himself, his head had been well thumped by a more practised hand.

This went on until a push at the door, and a "S—s! there's *sel'*," made all fly to their beds and out at the door like "snuffed dips."

By the time Jaw-ra-pa, the wardsman, got mounted up the two flats, the sleepers were snoring loudly, although he perhaps thought very breathlessly. Going into the wee ward, he turned up the gas, and seeing all were in bed put the light out. It is curious that it did not strike him as being strange to see them all sleeping so soundly on pillows only two thicknesses of cotton high, with all the stuffing at one end; but perhaps he had been relishing his supper and thought it was all right, and that the boys slept two in a bed.

On shutting the door and going into the fifth ward, where he had an enclosed portion for himself, they heard no more of him. After a minute or two the heads were raised from each bed in the wee ward, and, amid a great deal of smothered laughter, the pillows were shaken into their original shape. The fortunes of the combat were discussed, and particulars of some well-directed stroke, given or taken, were duly recounted. After this, sleep had been either driven from or had left their heads, so that the usual round of stories commenced.

The knap with the tale of the "Wark dug" tried to take advantage of the occasion, but it was no good; he was silenced at once.

One of the boys told about a knap who had been firing squibs, and "peoyes" on the Queen's birthday, when all his "pouther" blew up in his face; and how Meenie "rowed his heid in treacle clouts" until he was better. He was a long time in mending; possibly the quality of the ointment had something to do with it.

Another tale was told of an old joiner, named Belshie, who used to be on the premises. Some of the knaps made a habit of bringing in twist tobacco and giving him it, one of them playing a trick by handing him a piece of beautifully manufactured tarry rope. He received a blessing for it, but after Belshie had nearly broken his gums trying to bite a bit off, he almost broke the knap's head with a rake handle. Belshie complained bitterly to "Soo-Bode," who told him never to trust the "blecks," at least so far as "baccy" was concerned.

"Here, Mackay, tell us you story about the garriers. I heard you tellin' a bit o' it yae nicht."

"Oh aye," said Mackay, "that wis long ago, when it was the King's instead of the Queen's birthday, there used to be rare times in the town, an' generally the knaps had the maist hand in it. It was about the only time when they were on good terms with the apprentices, an' even with the keelies. They used to gether up for a long time before. When it wis near the time they wid hae excursions out to the Pentland Hills an' ither places, where they could get whins and bushes to decorate the auld wells and connies about the High Street. On the morning, early, they a' got out, an' some o' the auld callants that were guid hands at buskin' Geordie, had the job to deck the statue on horseback up in Parliament Square. The auld callants' club chaps had a' the keelies put up to nab flowers and evergreens, to the great torment o' the Links and 'Wark' 'green warriors,' funny sort o' sowls, dressed in long-tailed coats, white waistcoats, short breeches, and cocked hats. They were the bobbies in thae times, an' mony a race they used to hae after the wee fellows as they bolted in to the town wi' their oxterfu's o' plants.

"They used to hide them in cellars about the booths and auld houses that were in Parliament Square at that time, where they had the timber and stolen peats gathered up for the bon-fires. Early in the morning, long before the knaps got out, the callants wid be busy putting wreaths a' round the horse and down the big stane pedestal it was standing on, with a fine crown on Charlie's head, and his baton covered with fresh flowers in a way that made it look like a big "bookie." They were well up to their job.

"After a' was done, the bon-fires were lichted, and squibs, crackers, and 'peoyes' set off to ony quantity. As the day went on some rare fun got up. If onybody that they didna like came past, a' sort o' things were pitched at them—deid and livin' cats, rotten eggs, cod heads, and even sheeps' and calves' heads and feet were thrown about at onybody and everybody. The fun was carried on far into the night, but a' the knaps had to be in at a certain time, so that put a stop to their fun, though yin or twa o' them wad sometimes bolt for a' night.

"Yin, Jock Aitken, a wild sowl, wad get twa or three o' them to dae it in spite o' the govies and maisters; an' rare rows they kicked up among the towns-folk. There used often to be rare bats on the Saturdays. Sometimes the 'neets' and the knaps wid club thegither against the High School, an' proper bickers on the links and meadows wid be carried on. Vince when the 'neets' and knaps were busy at it themselves, the town rats or warriors made a rush at them, but the knaps an 'neets' shook hands and clubbed thegither and leathered the bobbies richt into the town."

Next morning some of the youngsters who had been in the pillow melee of the night before showed signs of having been at the front. One was quite lame, having, in rushing into his own ward, struck his foot on part of a stool which had proved the stronger, the lad having nearly broken his toe. It was very rare that those escapades were finished without some small accident.

During the day, as Walter and Ross were passing down to the well, they met Peter, the gardener, with the terrier under his arm, walking towards the Greyfriars gate.

On quizzing him about it, he said, "I've tried ower and ower again to put it out by the Vennel door, but it'll no gang, so I'm just gaun to try it at the ither side, and see if that'll dae ony guid."

They walked along with him, and when he came to the strong iron wicket, Peter opened it and pitched the dog quietly into the graveyard, where it took up its abode and apparently "took a notion to auld Brown the sexton fur a maister, and no being extra partickler for a draft o' wind as long as it was sheltered frae the wet, lay under yin o' the table tombstanes."

Through time it found its way into Traill's coffee-house, where the workmen used to feed it with bits of scraps, and strange to say it soon "learned to ken the *one o'clock gun.*" Walter was not very sure, but he thought old Brown called it "Bobby." However, it's dead now, and has a monument.

That night, after the hall (or tea time), the adventurers met and made the usual skirting preparations. Johnstone, Ross, Fowler, Walter, and Kidd made up the band; Sinclair could not come as he was confined for Cockie. Kidd was cautioned not to laugh too loud and spoil the thing.

Climbing one after another up the dyke, by the well-worn foot holes, Walter found himself on the T angle, where the old wife's garden wall met the shrubbery dyke.

Walking along a yard or two, it changed from stone-coping to brick, and, some of the bricks being loose, it was rather a ticklish job. But it was not far until a generous limb of the historic pear tree lifted the knaps into its bosom to regale themselves on the fruit. In truth, they might as well have taken one of the loose bricks as the hard unripe fruit, so far as their teeth were concerned, but the fact that it was stolen naturally made it more palatable.

On all getting into the branches, the pig-sty was pointed out to the new comers, almost right under the tree, built against the corner of the angle. The garden was rather more than half-an-acre in extent, with a quaint old house standing at the lower end. It was, or had been at one time, tastefully laid out in plots of flower beds; rows of dead gooseberry bushes spoke also of what had grown there in days gone by.

No doubt the old lady could not see the force of year after year tending fruit for the "vullains ower the dyke tae pluck."

After sitting quietly trying to mark some of the pears with their teeth, they heard the "grumph, grumph," from the ground floor tenant as he came out for an evening stroll within his limited space.

After a few more satisfied grumbles, which sounded somewhat between a whine and a bark, a well-aimed pear from the hand of Ross struck him on the side of the head. The stroke made him lift his fat sides like a pair of bellows, and when they fell it was with a noise something between a groan and a squeal. Cocking up his eye as well as his stiff neck would allow him, he beheld in his shady bower not only pears but yaps (beg pardon, knaps), and before he got into his shelter again the shower of bitter fruit made him talk rather freely in his own particular language, which no doubt was a string of blasphemous expressions.

Johnstone, stealing down the tree, got a piece of an old barrel stave with which he poked him up, and they had something like an African opera, the closing bars of which were heard long after they were back over the wall, now and then mingled with the contralto consolations of the old wife, who had appeared upon the scene, wondering what possessed her porker.

The order was given out that the Dancing class would commence on the next Friday, and Walter having passed over the second section and entered the third, his class was to have an hour of the "light fantastic." Walter was very glad to hear of it, as it would vary the monotony of the other classes on Wednesdays and Fridays. All the knaps liked "Gleedie." The only kind of tawse he ever used was his fiddle-bow, and he had snapped a number of them in this way, more to the amusement than the pain of the offender.

On the day mentioned, the third section went to the 'cond school in one of their play-hours, so that the dancing did not interfere with any of their other classes.

On Walter entering, he sat down with the rest of his companions. "Gleedie" had just arrived. He opened his press, which was at the back of the teacher's desk, and taking out his box, from which he took his well-known violin, he stuck it under his left arm, the hand grasping the neck. Standing in the centre of the floor in a stiff attitude, he looked round the room at his new class.

He was rather a peculiar old man, and had in the cut of his attire a very marked appearance as of a gentleman belonging to a past century. He wore a black-doeskin, claw-hammer coat, with trousers tapering slightly towards the boots. He had a peculiar cast about his eyes, so that when talking to one lad he would be looking at another, which often caused great fun. At his request all stood up, and each pronounced his own name in rotation, the name being carefully repeated by "Gleedie." This, with the fitting on of dancing pumps, taken from the press in which he kept his fiddle box, was about all the first lesson.

The next was heel, toe, shake, shift—preliminary positions for the Highland dancing; then the bend-jump for the Schottische; and bowing, setting, swinging, used in Quadrilles and other square dances. This was generally got over in about six lessons. Places for Quadrilles were called, and in turn the Lancers and Country Dances.

When trying to explain to his pupils the differences of reward which he would bestow for behaviour, "Gleedie" would march to the top of the line with a light springy step (although he was a heavy, stout man), and placing his hand gently on the first one's head, remark, "This is what I do to the good boys." To the next he would administer a rap on the side of the head, quite hard enough to make the boy's eyes water, while he remarked, "And that to the bad ones."

Another source of amusement to Walter was his admission into the "Wark" Band. Inquiries were made for some of the smaller boys willing to learn the flute, and Walter offering his services was accepted. He received a black ebony B-flat flute, with which he and the other recruits played firsts, seconds, or fourths, as it suited them, until they could manage the scale, at which stage they were allowed to take part in a march-out. Whether their efforts added to the harmony may be open to question, but they certainly managed to increase the volume of sound in a marked degree.

Now and again, the temper of the Band Instructor, at that time an old Teutonic gentleman, was sorely tried by some of the brass instruments coming in with a wrong note. Once when practising in the sixth school this happened. All he could do would not stop the discordant notes, proceeding from one of the small horns, which was in the hands of a wag of a fellow.

The old man stopped the band over and over again, making the horn player go over his part singly, in which he was perfect. "Try it vonce again. Come now: von, two, tree: ta, ta, ta-ta-ta, ta-ta-ta, ta-ta—shtop, shtop, vere did you got dat nodte, boy; tell me, vere did you got it?" There was likely to be a row by this time. The teacher was getting angry; the boys were warming for a bit of fun, and after another trial, instead of one false note, there were at least half-a-dozen.

This was too much for the musician's patience. Grasping his walking stick firmly, he laid on right and left, until the bandsmen were jumping about over the desks like cats. "Do you thought dat I come here to be made von fool for?" he inquired, and fixing his hat firmly on his head he walked downstairs, leaving the Band to its own meditations. This was his last appearance.

Walter, although a strong healthy lad, had been complaining at home of a certain sickness which sometimes seized him, and on his mother asking the doctor's advice, he was ordered to get cod liver oil.

The first taste was enough; once a week was bad, but night and morning were terrible to contemplate.

> "I'm sure ye've a' heard,
> Close on seven,
> A waesome cry, baith lang and even,
> Twa'd match a fishwife frae Newheven,
> It wis 'cod-ile';
> Which cry as soon as be believin',
> Ye'd rin a mile."

Just before the seven o'clock bell rang for the preparation class, if perhaps all were engaged romping in the class-rooms, or sitting in the parlours reading, the square was quiet. The one who had charge of the cod liver oil gobblers would station himself at the foot of the stairs at Mammie's connie, and in a long sing-song tone would cry, "Cod-ile, Cod-ile." The monitor did not cry long before the boys were running at top speed to be first up.

Not that they had any desire for the oil—far from that; but only, pity the hindmost; he had rare "milk" to drink. It was like taking a mouthful of "castor" to put away the taste of "cod." At this time there were about eighteen boys on the list. The first or second night Walter did not hurry, but he tried to be quicker afterwards.

They went up the stair, and on gaining the top they met Meenie posted in the little lobby outside of the sickroom door, with a small oblong table, on which burnt a feeble light in an old-fashioned brass candlestick. An antique blue-and-white jug, half-filled with milk, and a large square bottle of the oil were also on the table. It was not the fine, tasteless, cold-drawn emulsions we get now-a-days, but a strong, heavy liquid that had a most disagreeable taste. Although the knaps who were in the sickroom used freely to steal Meenie's acid syrup, no one was ever known to pilfer her "cod-ile." Yes, there was one, but he had made a mistake in taking the one bottle for the other, they being the same shape and size!

As the boys came forward to the table, about a quarter of a cupful was poured out and handed to each, one after the other. The "ile" went into his mouth, but if he was an old hand—well, he made pretence of drinking the milk. By the time all had been served the oil was reduced in quantity, but the milk—scarcely ever. Somehow or another it seemed to increase.

Two events of importance to the boys happened about this time. There was, first, the arrival of several long boxes filled with carbines, for the use of the boys while at drill; and, second, the arrival of a new wardsman.

A new wardsman was always looked upon with interest; he was so closely connected with the boys, and much of their happiness and comfort depended upon his considerate leniency. A wardsman had a great deal in his power; and if he were a hard, exacting man he could make at least those who were not his favourites extremely and everlastingly miserable.

The new wardsman, so far as they could judge, was one not inclined to give too much scope to his charges. He was tall, dark, heavy-moustached, not a bad-looking man, with a suspicious smile always playing round his lips. What was he before he came? A jailer! Oh, glory, happiness is ours! It was not long until the boys found that they had caught a tartar—or rather a tartar was about to catch some of them.

Many little odd trifles, which all other men passed over, this one did not—at least not to those who ventured to say a word on their own behalf. For a by-name they called him, very appropriately, "Sprat-Catcher."

Amongst his earliest schemes was a system of giving bad marks for very trifling offences. Those marks were exhibited on a board at the lodge window every Saturday morning. For every mark, one hour's confinement—seven being equal to the whole of Saturday. Any boy with ordinary spirits, anything above moping, could without much difficulty score about sixteen marks in a week, and still be well-behaved, his only fault being that he was not a favourite.

"Sprat" used to walk about with his little pocket-book, and mark, mark, mark, never telling the boy, knowing that he would see it all on Saturday *on the board.*

When in the parlours, perhaps for jumping across the long table, or standing on a form; being out of line in the square, in the green or school-room not belonging to their class, or romping as they always used to do without let or hindrance previous to his coming, down they all went—mark, mark, mark. Some who could very easily raise their average were made to pay the extras in various ways.

One way was by having them punished instead of making a mark against them, or by making them stand during their play-hours along the wall at the lodge door, back to it, face to it, on one leg, &c., while he, taking his walk round the pillars, would give as he passed the word, "change," at which they dropped the right and lifted the left leg. Added to this, they were often made to spread out their arms, which gave them the appearance of a cross.

These were hard times for the poor knaps, who dared not complain, without risk of having their punishment increased. One day the mother of one of the boys came to visit him, and the position just indicated was that in which she found her son. She went straight to the Doctor, and spoke her mind rather freely on the subject, after which the boys were not so often fixed in such a degrading attitude.

Ultimately, the Doctor got tired of having to confine the boys for really doing nothing wrong, but not wishing to break the system of marks, he made a rule that everyone who had no marks the week before should be allowed home on the Wednesday evening for two hours. This was good enough for those who could keep from the hateful marks; but as for Walter, Ross, and Co., it was as it had never been, Walter being out only once during the time "Sprat's" reign lasted, and that week "Sprat" was unwell.

CHAPTER XII.

THE dark evenings were beginning to come round again. The lamps in the square were lit about half-past five, and the parlours and schoolrooms soon after. Fires were kindled in most of the rooms, and the boys, as they crowded round the iron guards in front, were claiming the middle, next the middle, and so on. It was common enough on a chilly night to see five lads sitting on the top of the screen or large fire-guard, the others crowding round with their backs against it, so that not a spark of fire could be seen. All enjoyed the warmth, nevertheless. Stories and small talk went the round. Walter was one of the number. Ross appeared at the parlour door and beckoning to him, said, "Here, Crighton." Walter gave up his place next the middle to one of his friends (for you could dispose of your place if you chose, unless it were claimed by a lawd), and walked out to Ross.

"What's up?" he asked.

"Come on," said Ross, "we're gaun up to the 'cond school to hae a game at the 'Boar hunt.' This is a rare night for it," he added, blowing on his fingers and slapping them under his arms.

"A' richt," said Crighton, and over they went to the 'cond school. The lights were all up, and everything looked cheerful. About twenty boys were jumping about, and one or two of the kids were playing on the far-off window sill, at the back of the desks.

"Here, Johnstone, you and I'll 'chaps sides,'" cried Ross; "sherps or ends?" he said, holding a pencil within his hands.

Johnstone guessed wrong, so Ross took "first pick."

"I'll take Crawford."

"I'll take Tod."

"I'll take Wright."

"I'll take 'Speckie' Walker," and so on, until they were all ten-a-side, after which it was "sherps or ends for the outens" (or the privilege of being the boars). Ross' side lost; so mounting Walter on his back, and each one of his side doing likewise with a neighbour, the game commenced.

Johnstone and all his brother boars running about at first rather bewildered the horsemen, but after a little manœuvring and working well together several of the smaller ones were caught and crowned, which brought down the number to four. Johnstone, Fowler, Tod, and M'Gilvray gave the hunters some trouble in trying to secure them, but they were all caught except Johnstone.

He was a heavy-made lad, and had a deal of weight when he dashed through the mounted row of Nimrods. At last they got him into the corner at the door. Facing round, and turning up his coat collar, buttoning his jacket, and lowering his head, he made a rush as if for the centre of the attacking party. All closed up to him, but darting back he made a bolt for the end of the line which he turned, and then a fine chase ensued, round and round, keeping well into the centre, while they gathered themselves and again backed him into a corner.

Each one was heated and eager, the horsemen leaning to the right side, the arm hanging down, the left grasped tightly round the horse's breast, each knap watching closely the movements of the infuriated animal, which was snorting and pawing, making ready for a final rush. It came right in the centre, sending two of the number sprawling, which of course put them out of play.

Unluckily, he tripped up, and the remaining horsemen having firm hold of the lapels of his coat they jumped off their horses and proceeded to crown him.

This was giving him one, two, three, on the head; he was not crowned if his hand was on his head. A sharp struggle was made by the valiant animal, but crowned he was. This finished the "outens" of Johnstone's side. He arranged with his lads which of them were to be horses and which riders; and when time was called they mounted, and the new boars roamed at large.

All were caught after a little manœuvring, Ross being the last. He made the best show of the lot, making the remaining horsemen dismount and crown him twice, he struggling out of their grasp each time before they finally gave him the *coup de grace*. The weird, ghost-like cry of "cod-ile" from the square stopped the game; one or two of the number had to bolt—*to bolt* the horrid stuff.

Next day with the variorum of events came an agreeable change, the boys being informed before they left the chapel that it had been decided to take them to the evening performance at Quaglini's Grand Circus, which was stationed in the Lothian Road, opposite the end of Castle Terrace. This was, indeed, good news, and more so when the steward told some of them that Louege, the great flying trapeze wonder, was an auld callant.

The school-hours past, it was fast approaching the time for getting ready. Small groups of knaps were gathered here and there between the pillars and in the parlours, passing the time in professional gossip, giving personal experiences with the "Portie" cuddies, &c. One of the boys was heard to say that if it (that is the trapeze performance) looked anything easy, they should ask the govies to erect one in the shed, and get Mitchell to try it.

"Him try it!" said Campbell, with a scornful turn of the lip; "it wid be far ower birsy fur him."

"I believe he wid try it," added another; "he's aye blazing about what he can dae on the bar at the pend gate, and the gas-pipes in the 'cond school."

"He may dae well enough on the 'cond school pipes," said Cameron, "but he's ower buckin' fur to catch a trapeze; he wid fa' and breck his neck, an' a widna be gushing for him, the auld Mieser Doddie. He disna only miese his sock and chit, but even a' the pictures out o' his 'cricks.' Under his mattress is fair packed wi' them." (Here a general laugh broke the conversation.) "I tell you," continued the speaker, "the nugget's cakie, an' as big a sumph as is in the 'Wark.'"

"He's aye douchie baith in Billy's and Cockie's, and dirks almost everything he tries in his ither classes," remarked Patterson. Do you mind when he got the lick on the lug fur trying to dodge frae douchie to don to get off wi' his turn in Billy's?" (Here two or three "yakes" showed that the circumstance was remembered.) "Well, he turned a' buddies and seaas, and he said that wis what did it." Another laugh resounded through the square.

The bell rang, which sent the boys scampering up to the bolls to change their clothing, which being done, they mustered in the square and were marched by Lauriston Street and Grindlay Street to the circus. How they did enjoy it—what school-boy does not?—even the outside, with its large picture posters of horses flying through hoops, men in piles like Egyptian Pyramids, others balancing long poles with a companion seated on the top, ponies performing, and all the et ceteras, faithfully shown inside (if you liked to believe it).

But the great charm of the outside was the flaming and spluttering naphtha lamps, not only of the aristocratic Hippodrome itself, but of the many small side shows which followed in the wake of the larger establishment. Nor must we forget the tall man, seven feet eight inches high; the small one only thirty-six inches high; the fat lady, and the skeleton boy; the south-sea islander from the west of Ireland, the talking seal, and so on. Whenever a deformed person likely to raise curiosity was found, a new show was formed.

One fellow was standing at the door of his booth yelling to the astonished and gaping crowd at the top of his voice— "Hi, Hi, Hi; step in, ladies and gentlemen, step in, only one penny, that is all the charge for this night, gentlemen, all the charge for this night. Come and see the great lion-jawed Russian Prince, who has come from his own native land to exhibit his wondrous strength. You will never see the like again, gentlemen; only this once. Come and see for yourselves; this is the last opportunity you will have to see the man who lived upon the sinews and hides of wolves and hyænas, his only desire being to exhibit before you his wondrous strength of limb and jaw; and all for the small charge of one penny; a hero, gentlemen, a hero. Hi! Hi! now's your time, now about to commence. No waiting, no delay; everything shown on the outside guaranteed inside; this is positively the last time [he meant the poor prince who had to exhibit other twenty times that night], and as he goes by the first train tomorrow to keep an appointment with the Czar of the United States, the opportunity will never come again, gentlemen, never again."

As the boys passed, Walter thought that he should so like to see the wonderful prince and a few of his curious-looking neighbours; but by this time they had reached the inside of the Circus. Of course the lights were down, but after the band had finished the overture, a very bright arena presented itself.

Little Meers, the funny clown, and, in turn, Wallet, the Court Jester, gave some selections from his budget of quaint wisdom: but the interesting part for the knaps was just about to begin.

The bell was rung, and out came a tall, well-made fellow, dressed in a suit of dark tights. This was Louege, the Ariel Sprite. On reaching the centre of the ring, he made his well-calculated obeisance to the expensive seats, then turning to the gallery he looked for a moment or two and bowed to the knaps. I have no doubt his heart warmed as he beheld the rows of "wee short coaties," thinking of the time when he himself, with neither thought nor care, had played at the Boar Hunt and swung on the gas pendant in the 'cond school.

Mounting a high, raised platform, and having carefully rubbed his hands with resin, he sprang at the first bar. With a swing he left that and caught another, hanging above the centre of the arena; another swing and he caught a third, which landed him amongst his old schoolfellows (if I may call them so). After some wonderful feats of somersaulting and other performances, he finished his turn amid the hearty plaudits of all, especially the knaps.

When everything was over and they were on their way home, several of the parents and friends having heard that the boys had passed on their way to the Circus, were waiting for them, and some good pocks of "sock" changed hands. Others who had a few "maiks" to spare bolted into the small shops in Lauriston. Walter and Ross managed to secure a good stock of "gib" and some "bakes" for a "chip-in" when in bed.

On reaching the "Wark" a late supper was served, and after prayers in the Hall, the knaps passed up to the wards. After they were in bed, a good deal of "sock" munching and story telling went on, all being highly pleased with the trapeze swinging of the auld callant. Walter was satisfied long before he had finished his "gib" (or "gundy"), so he packed a number of the short broken lengths under his pillow to be disposed of in the morning, after which he fell asleep.

When the morning bell rang, and the rest were rising, he could not understand what held him so tight. Raising himself, not without an effort, he was horrified to find that his "gib" had somehow rolled down underneath him, and had melted by the heat of his body! His "chalker" and the under-sheet were completely glued together. After a little trouble, he got a separation. But what was he to do? Both his night-shirt and the sheet were spotted like a leopard's skin.

He called Ross, who laughed himself nearly into fits. Some of the others could not help noticing, and they, too, joined in the merriment at Walter's expense. Getting an old pocket knife, Ross and he scraped the sheet as well as they could, and then scrubbed it with a wet towel. For the remainder of the week Walter had to sleep on the spreckled bed, wondering all the time what the "wifie" who attended the ward would think. Right glad he was when a change of linen was made. Strange to say, however, most of the marks returned, even on this and the next one, always after it had been lain on for a night or two. Walter began to wonder how many copies the blessed mattress was going to throw off! It was a pity he and Ross did not think sooner to turn it over.

The chilly nights of November and December had come and gone, the Christmas holidays with their buns and shortbread; and a new set of kids had twice pushed out an old set of lawds. Several changes had been made in Wardsmen, Teachers, and "Wifies." Walter was now in the fourth ward and the fourth section, and was steadily rising in his position in the Square to the Chapel door. He was now in some new classes, such as Latin and drawing, was writing a fair "spacie," and was "creditable" in Cockie's.

That was a class-hour of the day which was almost universally liked amongst the boys. The room in which it was held was on the top floor of the north-east wing, corresponding with the sick-rooms and library in the others. It had two windows facing the north, and two looking into

Greyfriars. As you entered the door there was a small closet on the left, which held a countless number of broken slates, slate-frames, and tattered books, while the peg on the door sustained the teacher's coat and hat. On the right was the wee room, or, on the acting nights, the green room. Some plate-rack-looking shelving was fixed round it, into which each boy as he finished his lesson put away his slate, a compartment being assigned to each.

MATHEMATICAL CLASS ROOM—"COCKIE'S."

At the top of the class-room was a huge black-board that slid up and down between two posts, on which the sums were explained by the teacher. At the side of this was the teacher's desk with the knee-hole compartment where knaps used to hide from each other in their games of "seek." Four rows of cumbersome desks and seats running across the centre of the room, and a small mahogany table standing in the window, almost exhausted the inventory. We might perhaps add the big thick walking-stick, with a heavy silver ferrule, belonging to Cockie, in the west-most window. It was always a point of argument with the knaps whether it was a sword-stick or not. It ran many a narrow escape of having its head twisted off in trying to "prove it."

Cockie himself, a big man, was a kind master and a good teacher, and could gain credit by his pupils if they had the will in them at all. His peculiarity, as already indicated, was the manner in which he rubbed his fingers and pushed the point of his tongue out and in rapidly, and repeated the word "Aye! Aye!" when calculating or correcting the sums of the boys. There was hardly one of them who could not imitate him to a certain degree, some perfectly.

If a sign were wanted to prove an auld callant, this one would do, along with the mark "R," which always covered a sum if it was correct. He kept a pair of tawse like the other teachers, and used them too, but it was a very serious offence if the number of stripes exceeded three. A knap did not require to warm much for him, as his stripes were always lumpy, and dusted the cuff of the lad's jacket rather than struck his hand.

The English class was of a somewhat different kind. The knaps called it the "killing house." Boys at day schools who think themselves severely punished because they get the tawse, make a great mistake. It is not one man in twenty who can administer the "oil of strap" unless he has made it a particular study, and has the heart to lay it on. The use of the tawse is a science for which every teacher is not adapted, either from want of taste or lack of agility. It is not the strong arm and the weighty smack which have the greatest effect in the giving of pain; it is the sharp, quick stroke of the single tail, delivered either on the front or back of the hand, as the giver sees the poor little culprit about to flinch. There is no chance of "cutting" it with a man who can wield the leather in that way.

> "Ye'll mind lads how we used tae skirl,
> As — - gied his tawse the twirl,
> An' brought them down wi' sic a birl,
> True to the mark.
> Nae tawie science could compete wi' his
> In a' the ' Wark '."

We were often told what was "worth remembering," but the taste of the 'cond school tawse will not escape the memory very readily any more than the hated remark, "I'll take it on Saturday."

Simpson's Drawing class was held in the writing-school. It was one which the boys liked well enough. Each got a book of about twenty pages to be filled up with lines, circles, leaves, vases, and the usual things given to beginners to copy. After that was finished, a drawing-board and a large sheet of rough paper were given, and the choice of either mechanical, architectural, or free-hand drawing.

Most of the boys, I think, rather preferred free-hand, especially when any old "crockles" of the "doses" (which were got for rubbing-out purposes) were lying about, and Simpson's silk hat was standing in a good position for a "cock-shy." The knaps were really heartless at such a time; even their own companions have been forced to make an extra piston rod in some well-outlined engine, or to put an extra half-flat on a house, when one of the said crusts was thrown against the end of his pencil, much to his annoyance.

The next run was up to the seventh school, where the Dominie was waiting to explain his "Hic, Haec, Hoc."

He was passable when not in a "birse," when his hair had not been rubbed the wrong way. If he had been crossed, then it was the verbs, Gerund, Dum, Di, Do Dum, wanting Do. The "wanting" was generally supplied with a stout little cane, while he held the middle finger of your hand.

One of his favourite themes was connected with a strong mason, named Balbus, who built a wall; but whether they used bad lime, or from whatever cause, Ross, Crighton, and Co., could never get that wall built strong enough, unless, perhaps, on the day that Dominie got his "dibs"; then they could make him twirl his spectacles, and peacefully smile at their attempt.

The bell for dinner generally brought this class to a finish, and so the boys could console themselves over their "tout soup" and roast.

CHAPTER XIII.

THIS particular day being the first of Hallow Fair, it was arranged to bolt at night over to the Grassmarket, and have a whack at the ponies. It was easy enough getting over and back, but the trouble was with the Heriot Bridge keelies, who always lay in wait for the knaps and as likely as not caught them. However, they would run the risk. Moreover, there was to be a concert in a school in the West Bow, to which some of them had been invited.

It was in connection with a night-school class, and the teacher of the school was not aware that they were coming by any other than legitimate means. However, it did not matter as they could easily enough be back in time.

Bolting down the shrubbery from the east-most end, and climbing over the dyke into a little green on the other side of the auld wife's garden, they again mounted and dropped from a low wall into a dark yard, which had communication with the Heriot Bridge by an entry.

On leaving the entry, Ross proposed that they should go down two or three at a time, as they would not attract so much notice. Johnstone, Sinclair, and Kidd went first; Walter, Ross, and another lad, named Tommy Mice, followed; and two more, Murray and Clements, brought up the rear, making eight in all. When they reached the bottom of the hill, the market was about empty of horses; at least it was not in the packed state it had been during the day. A goodly number of ponies were galloping up and down, and the knaps busied themselves "chugging" their tails in view of hair (fishing) lines, which was with them almost as great an article of industry as balls. One of the hair lines made by Harvey was worth something.

Up the right hand or south side of the market towards Candlemaker Row were a number of stalls, the attendants of which were busy selling gingerbread and nuts. Some of the stall-keepers were exposing large coloured wheel-targets and spring guns, with which the youths of the city were firing darts, a lucky or good shot being rewarded with a handful of nuts, &c. After spending a few coppers in this way, the boys took their way up towards the West Bow. Passing the little sweetie shop, known as "Katie Flips," on the left hand side as you entered the West Bow, a few more coppers were spent on the toffies which bore Katie's name, and which were great favourites with the knaps.

Going further up and round the corner, they went on until they arrived at the Church which stands in the centre of the south side of the street; here, turning down a close, they entered a gate at the bottom, on their left. As they came to the door, Ross reminded Johnstone that he had promised to bring his flute, on which he was a very creditable performer.

"Oh, that's a' right, it's in my pocket," was his answer; "and mind some o' the rest o' ye 'll need to sing something."

On entering they saw a party of young lads and lassies, who had been attending the Evening Class during the quarter. They greeted the arrival of the Heriot contingent very cordially, the teacher never suspecting that he was welcoming a batch of runaways. One of the young ladies sang in a very pleasing manner a song which was popular at that time, entitled "Beautiful Isle of the Sea," after which Johnstone gave a very good selection of Scottish airs on his flute. Sinclair was next called upon, and he being considered the best endowed vocalist amongst the visitors, with grand style and action warbled out another popular ditty, called "The Calico Printer's Clerk," the chorus of which ran—

"She was very fond of dancing.
But allow me to remark,
That one fine day she danced away
With the Calico Printer's Clerk."

This was taken up and sung heartily by the happy party. It was followed by a song, "Kathleen, your going to leave me," by the twin sister of the first-mentioned fair vocalist, who sang very well. After some other attempts, the knaps had to take a hasty leave of a really enjoyable gathering and scamper back to the "Wark." Going straight down the close, they found themselves at the junction of the Candlemaker Row and the Cowgate, and turning down the Grassmarket they made for the Heriot Bridge. When they came to the bottom, they were rather startled by a little fellow bolting up, and shouting at the top of his voice—"Here's the Heriotties, here's the Heriotties."

"What's to be done now?" said Sinclair; "look up, there's about twa dizzen waiting for us." And sure enough about half-way up a batch of rough boys were waiting, as they knew too well, for their return.

"We'll be better tae gie them our sock and be done with it," said Clements.

"No' very likely," responded Ross, fiercely. "I'll be hanged first."

"Same here," came from the rest of them.

"I'll tell you what," said Ross, "you gang up first, Tommy, and if ony o' them stops you and asks for sock, just whistle Heriottie, and we'll make a rush for it."

This was agreed to. Tommy went slowly up and was just about to pass them when two or three stepped in front and stopped him. They were evidently going to "ripe," as one caught him by the collar, and two others got his hands. Upon this he whistled quickly.

"I kent it," said Ross; "keep thegither and bash through them." Up they went, double trot, right at the centre of the group, never stopping to have words, Ross striking the biggest one right in the mouth and rolling him into the gutter. This was the signal for a free fight, but the knaps kept well together and fought in earnest. In about five minutes all the pluck was out of the keelies, the well-aimed blows of the knaps telling upon some of their dirt-begrimed noses. At last they turned and fled down the bridge, followed part of the way by the knaps. Ross called them back, and they all hid in the entry. "Wait here for a minute," he said; "they'll come back and we widna hae time to get ower the dyke."

Waiting in the back part of the entry, as true as he had said, up came the keelies, helter-skelter. Out they went again in the same way, for the knaps were among them in a twinkling, and gave it to them even warmer than before.

"Now," said Ross, as soon as they had taken to flight the second time, "up the dyke as hard as you can."

"Have ony o' you got hurt?" he asked, as they got up to the well.

"My nose has been bliddin'," said Sinclair.

"And mine, tae," added Kidd; "but ne'er mind if there's nae 'keekers'."

The marks of the combat were of course washed off at the well, and all were safe for the time.

The ward our friends were now in was what was called the fourth ward, looked after by the steward, Shinnie, and as he left for home after all were (or as he supposed) asleep, a good deal of liberty was taken. The monitor, Graham, was a very quiet-going chap, and could not very well control such a set of noisy fellows as were under his care. The steward had a little terrier. It was a general favourite with all the boys, but, notwithstanding that, they could not help playing a trick upon the dog when an opportunity occurred. When his master was working at his accounts at the table in front of the fire, "Clyde" would sometimes take up his quarters on the foot of the monitor's bed, and he often got a friendly pat from the lads in passing. They all liked to pat Clyde and he liked to be patted; in fact, he was a "good dog, Clyde."

The boys occasionally brought in some pepper with them for their kail, but as the quantity supplied by the cook was considered sufficient, the steward (and no doubt he had a stern reason) would not allow it to be used, and confiscated it whenever he found it in their possession. This displeased them very much, and so one night as poor

Clyde was lying sleeping on Graham's bed, one of them taking a pinch of pepper quietly laid it on the coverlet in front of the dog's nose. All got into bed and awaited the result. The first effect was a snort, then another, then a succession of about a dozen snorts which made Clyde's master stop his calculations in order to see what he was about. "Clyde!" His only answer was to jump to the floor and run madly from one end of the ward to the other, with his nose rubbing the ground, only stopping to shake his head, as at other times he would shake his tail.

"Who's been meddling with the dog?" asked the steward.

No one had been near him; the monitor could verify the statement, for all had been in bed some time. It was a good while before Clyde came to himself, as the pepper was rather stronger than the ordinary kind; and the lad who gave it said he did not think it would be so bad, as it was called "Canine" pepper.

When the steward had gone, and all were supposed to be sleeping, a good joke was proposed—to tie on the monitor a wifie's night-cap which they had found at Mammie's door.

The monitor was sleeping, so turning up the gas and going up to his bed they managed to cap him and tie the strings neatly under his chin. Ross now supplied himself with a towel soaked in water, and crept under the monitor's bed; other two of his cronies took their bowsters and stationed themselves on either side of the bed. "Ready! one, two, three," and down came the bowsters on Graham's head.

After collecting himself and sitting up, he put his hand on his head, wondering no doubt whether he was dreaming or if he really had the "kell." It was some time before he got the knot untied, and during the process he kept lecturing the boys upon what they would receive on the morrow. During his speech, Ross quietly deposited the wet, sloppy towel on his bed; and Graham, having exhausted his threats, flung himself down, only to rise again nearly mad with fright and rage. By this time all the boys were awake and enjoying the fun.

Presently a voice, as from the ceiling, said, "Now then, we've been watching all through this lark, or game, or whatever you may call it. You've finished it pretty well; go to sleep, and let this be the end of it."

On looking up the boys saw Levick's head and shoulders sticking out of a small window in a trap-stair which came down from his ward. After this they lay quietly down to sleep, never thinking that they would have something to alarm them before the night was over.

About half-an-hour had passed, and all were sound asleep, when the terrible cry of "Fire! Fire! Fire!" rang through the "Wark." The shouting and thumping overhead awoke all the boys, who were soon sitting on their beds as frightened as could be. They heard the door opening hurriedly, and a quick step coming through the washing-house.

Sprat looked in and cried, excitedly, "Every boy pick up his clothes, tuck them under his arm, and get downstairs."

On reaching the square, they found the boys of the fifth, sixth, seventh, and eighth wards there already. Never before had there been such a gathering of "chalkers" in the square.

"Where is the fire? Where is it?" asked the fourth ward boys.

"Do you not see it up there, in Levick's ward?" was the retort.

They went over to the hall side, where they saw the flickering light of what might have been a serious fire being got under by the application of wet blankets. The square had rather a motley appearance; some were drawing on their socks, others their trousers; all, however, seemed

"FIRE! FIRE!" OFF TO LONDON.

to be enjoying the affair as a good lark. One of the officials belonging to the building department had been sent for, and when he arrived both boys and wardsmen got it all round, and in strong language, too.

The cause of the fire was a leaky gas-pipe, which was carried along the ceiling of the ward. So strong was the smell that the servants had been endeavouring to find the leakage and temporarily stop it. For this purpose a light had been applied, and the pipe, a lead one, melted, so that in a few minutes the whole ceiling was enveloped in flames.

One incident of the fire rather tickled the knaps. Sidney, one of the London boys, was so frightened, that instead of staying with his companions, he bolted down to the front gate at Lauriston with his clothes under his arm, not taking time to put on even his socks. In great terror, he implored Mrs Levick to let him "go 'ome"; whether he meant to take the train direct, or whether he had friends in town is not known.

The result of the fire was that the seventh ward boys had to sleep with the fourth ward ones. It was rather a crowded arrangement, but it varied the monotony. However, it did not last long, as in a day or two everything was put right.

Some of the evenings were made instructive and amusing by a series of lectures from Mr Page, the geologist, and other lectures on various subjects. One night an exhibition rather than a lecture was given by a foreign gentleman upon the subject of musical instruments, the lecturer imitating the tone of the different instruments by the mouth alone.

Another instructive amusement was an astronomy class taken up by "Cockie." All knaps who wished could attend. The first night on which the class met was clear and bright; all the stars glittered like diamonds. Every class-night there was about an hour's work pointing and explaining; and in a few lessons a good idea of the more important stars and constellations was got by the boys. There were the Pole Star, the Plough, the Great and the Little Bear, the Charioteer, the Lady in her Chair, Venus, Mars, and Jupiter, and many others which they could recognise and point out to some of the younger ones.

The Christmas holidays had come and gone in the usual way, and the lads who were fortunate enough to possess a pair of skates were scrubbing them up on the stone flags under the pillars to make them as sharp as possible for coming events, for, with the return of the boys, came hard frosty weather.

A good black frost was always a delight as it allowed them to have grand long slides from the centre of the square to the "connies." The wardsmen had received orders to water the square on the east side; and attaching the hose to the plug in the centre, they soon ran it all over, and after repeating the process two or three times a very serviceable sheet of ice was formed.

It had the whole day to freeze, and after tea it was in excellent trim for skating. In reality, a grand nights fun was obtained. The parlour lights were all lit, casting from the windows a bright glare over the improvised pond. The long slides carried a constant stream of knaps, sliding straight into the sixth school stair, and running round the pillar, taking the other slide to Beddie's "connie." Those were the nights of downright enjoyment; good ice, and no fear of a ducking; a health-deriving sport, full of fun, which makes one look back and long for a return of the jolly evenings when the shout was, "Keep the puddin' hot."

The Doctor also told the man to have the shed watered, as he thought a good sheet of ice might be formed there for skating in the daytime. The knaps themselves carefully covered the flat at the bottom of the 'ird green stairs with water.

Next day the frost was as hard as ever, and the shed was well taken advantage of. The Doctor now informed the boys that if the frost continued as hard on the morrow, he would have them taken down to St Margaret's Loch. This was good news, and many a heart-felt wish was uttered for the continued reign of King Frost. At night the knaps put patent thermometers, namely, porringers full of water, out of the bedroom windows. In the morning they were delighted to find them as hard as iron.

At twelve o'clock they got ready and had their dinner early. Several of the lawds got their "fags to pouch" for them, and as it was cold roast that was an easy matter. Everyone who could manage it had a 'cond share, and there was a good deal of "squeezing of pouches" you may be sure. Several of the younger knaps came to grief, as the older ones gave the order, "Skin doses," which deprived many of their "chit" who were not smart enough to pick it off the table.

When they got into marching order, the word was given, and all went merrily out by Greyfriars, Lothian Street, and Drummond Street, to the Queen's Park. A goodly number of people were already on the ice, and before long the boys were skating and sliding in infinite enjoyment along with the throng. There were one or two stands where biscuits, lemonade, coffee, and "sock" were being sold, and a good few coppers were spent on these commodities. There were some good skaters amongst the boys who "lambed it" to their heart's content, and created no small amount of envy among those who had no skates. With some this matter of skates was a joint-stock concern; that is to say, there were boys with one a-piece, on which they slid gaily along, perhaps more safely than they would have been able to do on two.

Walter and Ross had each a pair of very good skates, but unfortunately they were badly supplied with straps, and it was with difficulty they could be made to stay on. When Walter was not skating he took great delight in watching the evolutions of one man with long, brown leather leggings. His skates were of a very peculiar make, the toe of the steel rising about six inches with a graceful sweep in the shape of a swan's neck. He was in truth a most accomplished skater, and was, in the opinion of the knaps, the "Lamb of the Loch."

The long slides were well patronised. Small boys and tall boys, men and girls, short soldiers from the Castle and long ones from Piershill, errand lads with baskets and others with parcels, even one or two sailors—all were following one another in motley procession, waving their arms, and shouting "Keep the puddin' hot." Occasionally the tail end of the slide would present rather a mixed gathering of the human species, all in a heap, which made great fun and caused much laughter for those on the bank who dared not venture, as well as for the sliders when they had picked up and identified themselves.

The afternoon wore on, and the daylight drew in; then the whistle was sounded. All were making for the east side of the loch where Doctor Bedford was standing, when a sharp cry was heard from somewhere about the centre. The people stopped their careering and gathered round someone who had fallen.

"What is the matter?" asked the Doctor of a gentleman who was coming hurriedly over.

"One of your boys down, sir." answered the man, "and I think rather severely hurt."

By this time three or four persons were carrying one of the lads between them.

"Who is it? Who is it?" resounded on every side.

As the boy was laid in an unconscious state on the bank, they saw it was Sinclair. The rest of the boys looked first at his pale face, almost as white and lifeless as the snow on which he was lying, and then at the troubled expression of the Doctor as he waited to hear the opinion of a medical gentleman who happened to be on the spot. They crowded together in almost breathless silence. After a pause of about a minute, during which the gentleman was pressing and working about the prostrate lad's body, he rose up and, turning to the Doctor, reported that there was rather a serious fracture of the collar bone.

"He will require to be very carefully removed," said the medical gentleman.

Poor Sinclair was laid on a bed made of the knaps' capes, which were spread out on the snow until a cab arrived. He was then rolled in one of the large brown capes, and cautiously lifted into the vehicle, the Doctor and one of the warders taking seats beside him.

After a tiresome and silent walk, the knaps reached the "Wark." They went straight into the hall, and being ravenously hungry soon finished their allowance of "chit and milk." On inquiring about Sinclair, they were told that he was very seriously hurt, but that he was not in a dangerous state, if only he were kept quiet.

At night, in the ward, several stories went round, some about accidents which had formerly taken place in the "Wark." One story was told about a knap who had a nightmare. He went out of one of the windows on the east side of the square, and when the steward arrived in the morning there he was sitting astride the top of the "leads." Unfortunately the man not knowing the meaning of the eccentricity called loudly to him, and the boy, suddenly waking, rolled down, fell to the gravel, and was killed.

A heavy snowstorm having set in, the usual liberties were given, although not quite to the same extent as before, owing to the watchful vigilance of "Sprat," who made it "warm" for any boy whom he regarded as going in the slightest over the line. However, the tellers were "housed," and some fine bickers were indulged in.

About this time some of the Parliamentary elections were going on, and one of the candidates had evidently greatly incensed the boys, for all over the place there was written in large chalk letters, "*Vote for M'Laren and Miller. Kick out Black the keelie.*" On copy books, on newspapers, wood partitions, in fact, anywhere that a lead pencil or chalk would show, there it was. It was not often that elections of any kind disturbed the equanimity of the "Wark" inhabitants, but this election did; and an order was issued, stating that any boy found disfiguring the walls would be severely punished. This stopped the chalking business, but the evidences remained for many a day.

CHAPTER XIV.

THE drill with the new carbines on the Saturday mornings was looked forward to as a great novelty. In each of the parlours there had been put up two cabinet presses, neatly fitted inside with a place for each "piece," and notches in which the bayonets hung.

As the boys presented themselves, they were handed a carbine and bayonet, which they soon learned to "shoulder" as smartly as any volunteer in the country. One morning Levick had applied to the Doctor for leave to "double" the boys out of the grounds; and permission having been granted, they were soon marching down the centre of the avenue towards Lauriston, four deep, with guns at the "long trail." As they passed through the gate they got the command, "Right turn: Shoulder arms!" A number of workmen who were passing rather stared at the little army on the march at such an early hour. They looked as if they did not know whether to laugh or take the matter seriously.

"Attention there! Left turn"; and the leading party turned down Wharton Lane. Marching them right across the West Meadows and up the Links as far as the Nunnery, then crossing to the centre of the green, the instructor put them through several battalion exercises, such as:

Form square on No. 1 Company; fire a volley, front rank kneeling; and 60 or 70 hammers came down with a bang. Then the irregular firing was rapidly done. "Cease firing: Attention! Fix bayonets: Shoulder arms: Form companies: Extend into line: Port arms: Charge bayonets: Charge!"

Away they went at the "double," down the Links and right through the Tumbler's Hollow, to the consternation of a band of golfers, who were preparing for a long drive, and who picked up their balls and clubs and bolted in the face of, as they thought, an advancing foe.

By the right, over hill and dale went the gallant and valiant Knaps' Brigade in search of an enemy, until the railings brought them to a standstill.

A tree happening to be in line with one of the front rank, before the word "halt" was called, there was such a willing thrust that it was with difficulty the blade could be got out and in a bent state. After a few minutes of "Stand easy," the quick march was resumed across the Meadows, up Wharton Lane, and home.

When they had piled arms, there never was assembled a squad of soldiers in better form or readier to attack plates of "pot" than were the knaps. The Doctor was well pleased with the result of the exercise, and Levick was empowered to take the boys out when the mornings were suitable. Sometimes a good long "double" was taken round Morningside district. On two or three occasions the whole of the boys were conducted out to the Links, having a "bist" or football with them, and an hour was spent on the frost-covered turf.

In one of the kids' parlours just above the fire-place were two little holes, where, evidently, at one time gas-jets had been. Two of the boys, thinking to have a lark, filled one of the holes with pieces of paper, and others having pushed pieces in at other times, quite a collection of sundry scraps had gathered inside the little orifice. The opening was small enough outside, but being behind wood-lining it was roomy enough inside. The boys thought it held a wonderful quantity and would take such a time to pick out.

After considering the matter, however, they concluded that a light applied to the hole would be the easiest and quickest way to get rid of the contents, and what would it matter supposing the "Wark" did go on fire. The light was applied accordingly. At first there was a little blaze; then the flames burst out anew, but to their consternation this time in a different place, coming through the wood.

Very soon the fire had assumed alarming proportions; and the now-frightened youths were running from the parlour with shouts of "Fire!" This brought the warders, who immediately sent to the shed for Muscle Doo. In the meantime they stripped off the lining, but the flames were tearing and leaping up between the wall and plaster. When Muscle Doo arrived he made his way up to the fourth ward, and breaking the wall he poured water copiously down behind the plaster. The fire was ultimately got under, and all danger was at an end. A gas-pipe had evidently melted and the gas taken hold, so that the fire might have been really serious if prompt measures had not been adopted. The two knaps were punished, but very little was said about the matter.

One morning a number of lads were congregated round the parlour door, laughing and evidently arguing about something. On Walter and Ross going up, they found one or two engaged at almost the only gymnastic game in the place, namely, jumping up and catching the lintel of the door with their hands, and pulling themselves up as often as possible. One had managed to get up a record of ten times, and no one, it was said, could beat that.

"Come on, Ross," shouted one of the group; "Scott can beat you here; he can pull himself up oftener than you."

Walking forward, Ross asked the number that had been made, and was told. Then he jumped at the small projection, and not only beat the "record" by two, but after numerous trials by other would-be gymnasts, he still stood victor.

"I can lick you at jumping the green stairs onyway," said Scott. "I can dae three-seven, an' that's what you canna."

"Go on an' try him," was the general chorus, and to the delight of all, Ross took up the challenge. The party made their way out to the front of the "Wark," and gathered on the stairs, leaving a space down the centre for the match.

"Will we begin frae the fit?" asked Scott.

"Begin at four," said Ross.

Going half-way down (there being ten steps), Scott jumped, Ross following. This was just by way of a preliminary; the next was five, then came six, followed by six-four, when Scott gave his flying leap of three-seven. Ross, although he had never tried the jump, without hesitation bounded after him, amidst the applause of the onlookers. Scott was rather annoyed. Apparently he was willing to hold the result as equal, but not so Ross. Fired by the applause of his school-fellows he went at it again. Running up the steps and taking a short run, he gave a splendid two-eight.

"There's for you, Scott; try an' lick that if you can," cried the boys.

Scott went up, and taking a long look at the second top step, made a run and also cleared two-eight. Ross laughed good-naturedly, and once more mounting to the top did a difficult jump of eight-two. This Scott also managed. One-nine was next done by Ross, but Scott's courage had failed him: he would not try it, although he faced it up several times. "Go on, Ross, go on an' dae a' the stairs." Perhaps he had a little fear, perhaps not; at any rate he succeeded in clearing the flight of ten steps beautifully, only, after having landed, he fell and, skidding amongst the gravel, skinned the palms of his hands severely.

"Never mind, Ross," said some of his sympathising backers; "there's no' anither knap can dae a' the stairs, an' only twa o' the lawds ever went clean ower them."

It was a good long jump for a boy, and certainly wanted nerve as well as agility.

It was Friday, and after having had their "pea-claw, touts and cone," they were busy with a game of "prisoner's base." Sometimes it was called "Scotch and English," but a more frequently used and a never-to-be forgotten name among the knaps was "Relieve-o." A den was fixed upon, and sides were chosen. One side went roving, the other went hunting for prisoners. Say the sides were eight each, and the "inside" had captured seven. One lad who was still at large, would make a rush for the den, and once getting his foot in he would cry "Relieve-o," when the whole seven were at liberty to bolt. Thus he would give his side a new existence, much to the annoyance of those in the den, since all their work was to be done over again.

They had had a good game, although a high wind had been rising and apparently was getting stronger. Going out to the balusters, Ross and Walter observed a number of the kids amusing themselves, holding up by the corners their large red handkerchiefs, the wind filling them like the sails of a ship, and driving the boys backwards. This was on the top of the terrace in front of the hall windows. There was no doubt that the wind was gathering in force, fast and furious, for one little fellow who had not time to reef got lifted off his feet, over the baluster pillars, and was laid down in the 'ird greens. This had the effect of making the whole "fleet" tack for the pend gate.

As the afternoon advanced, a fearful storm was in progress. Not one of the boys could go outside; and from the windows the trees could be seen raising their earth-covered roots in the air, fairly torn out of the ground.

Curiously enough, Peter the gardener and his assistant, Alec, were busy sawing and uprooting trees to open the front view of the Hospital to Lauriston, so that the twenty or more trees which were blown down just suited their convenience. About half-past four there came a terrible gust, which did a great deal of damage. It lifted the roof off the shed, which was of corrugated sheet-iron, about seventy-five feet long by sixteen wide, right over the turning-house, and laid it with a smash in the

Doctor's croquet green. Matters were really getting alarming; and the knaps were glad to "sneak" into the parlours and class-rooms, each furious gust making a pause in some story of horror and danger which was being told by some lover of fearsome anecdote.

Next day it was reported that much damage had been done all over the town. The top flat of a house in Duke Street had been blown in, and any number of chimney-cans, slates, "auld wifes," &c., were littered about the streets. One old tree stump in the "Wark" grounds, which went by the name of "Geordie's tree," was so shaken that it had to be propped up, and so it remained for many a day. It stood on the west side of the gate-house in Lauriston.

One morning when Walter reached the square he was accosted by Ross.

"Hallo, Crighton, big Simpson wants you; it's something about a French and Latin dictionary that he has lost. A knap telt him you kent where it was."

"Me? I ken naething about it," said Walter.

"Well, you'll better gang and see him, for he is in a proper birse," responded Ross.

Walter went on the hunt for Simpson, and having found him in the parlours, asked him what about his French or Latin book. At first Simpson stared blankly at him, but, as if recollecting, he said, "Oh yes, Ja-ra-pa in the Lodge lost yin. He says you had it last, an' he's rather anxious about it."

"Me? I couldna read it though I had it."

"Well, you'll better gang and see him aboot it yoursel'."

Away went Walter, and going into the lodge he found Ja-ra-pa sitting reading the morning paper.

"Simpson says you've lost a French book on Latin, an' you think I've got it," said Walter.

"What's that?" said Ja-ra-pa. "A French book on Latin?" and his eye catching the date on the top of his paper (April 1) as his ear caught the curious question, he remarked, "Oh aye, ye'll better see the cook, it's her that's lost it, and she swears you've got it."

THE LODGE—FIRST OF APRIL.

"Which one?" queried Walter; "the big or the wee yin?"

"Oh, the big cook; ye'll better see her at once."

Walter wondered what the cook wanted with either a French or a Latin book. Walking right into the kitchen he found the cook very busy and very warm, with a long pole, one end under her arm, the other in a large boiler of "pot."

"I say, cook, have you lost a book?"

"A fat's that!"

"Have you lost a French book on Latin that I'm blamed for having had?"

"Tuts, man," said the cook, "wha sent you tae me? It's Mr Robertson wha's lost the 'strange book on mutton'; ye'll find him in the store."

Walter passed out of the kitchen, scratching his head and thinking to himself that this was a most curious book which was lost and yet no one would claim it. When he entered the store, Robertson was busy cutting the "doses" for breakfast. As Walter approached, "Clyde" gave a yelp; the steward turned sharp round, and in his short brusque manner demanded, "Well, sir?"

"The cook sent me about a book you've lost about French on Latin, or something like that."

The steward stared at him for a second or two, and then asked, "What have I got to do with French or Latin either? If any more of you come here with your 1st of April jokes, I'll have you over to the lodge." Walter waited to hear no more, and bolted out of the store, his face as red as fire.

On entering the square, quite a gathering awaited him, with very civil inquiries about the cook's French book on Latin. Walter very wisely laughed it off, although he felt rather taken down with his stupid message. When he met Ross, the latter apologised for giving him a "gouk's errand," but explained that to make up for it he was going to give Beddie and Mammie one each after Chapel. Handing Walter a paper figure of a man and a crooked pin, Ross instructed him to fix it to Mammie's gown as she passed out of Chapel. He himself had a lady to fix on the Doctor's back. Both jokes were very successfully managed (indeed, the Doctor had more than one adornment), the paper figures being carried home to the several apartments of those who had thus been fooled.

June Day with the ball-making and band practising, &c., passed happily. The July holidays soon came round again, this time bringing several changes in the Hospital. Some of the places had been altered. The boys' head-gear was changed. For the small black leather peak a large projecting peak was substituted. These were the "cheese-cutters," horrible things with weight enough of thick heavy leather in front to round the shoulders of every boy who had to wear them.

A new book room was fitted up at the bottom of the sixth school stair; and some of the class-rooms got desks of an improved kind. The seventh school was altered, and re-named the lecture room.

A splendid moveable bronze rail was fitted round the inside of the Chapel door, so that visitors could only get thus far and no further, for what reason we could not learn.

A new set of lawds and kids, new wards and new classes, new monitors and often new companions, new wardsmen and (this was the ticklish part) new masters. What a speculation was a new master! Was he a "birsy yin!" What kind of a "taw" did he keep? Did he burn the ends, or dip them in whisky? Was he a "rare sowl?" Did he sometimes tell stories? No teacher was more thought of than he who could tell a good story while he taught. This time there was both a new wardsman and a new teacher. The wardsman was a six-foot giant, a very good fellow: "Lang Jamie" he was called. A good canny soul was Jamie. The teacher, who was named Bob, was one whom the younger boys appeared to like very well. So far, he had had only the younger classes under his charge, so that the rest could not form an opinion of him. He had shown his "taw" at once, but had never yet employed it much.

Our young friends had shifted into the 'ird ward, which was situated on the second floor of the north-west wing. It was what was called one of the "wee wards," not because of its being small, but rather because the one on the same flat was of the largest. It was on the same floor as the writing-school, and contained about twenty beds. Unfortunately, Ross and Walter were far apart; in fact, in opposite corners. However, it could not be helped.

One consolation was, that a good job had fallen to the lot of Ross. A lawd who had gone out left one of the "fat cribs" of the institution to him, namely, to clear the stove on the kitchen flat when any extra quantity of warm water was wanted by the cook, and on all mornings when the bath had to be used the same night. This happened four mornings a week. Ross had to choose a partner, and, of course, Walter was the one.

You may ask—What was there in clearing the stove? The clearing was the least of it. All you had to do was to "spur," and then pass out as soon as dressed down to the stove, draw forward one of the large iron buckets, shove a long iron raker into the stove, and pull out the ashes; take a handle each, and carry the bucket out to the front of the pend gate ready for the carts to remove, and the job was done. Then, a seat at the big blazing kitchen fire, with "chit and butt," cold roast or cheese, and a cup of good tea—this was something in G. H. H.

Another new position which Walter got was the second place in the precentor's "box," with a salary of two-and-sixpence a year (Mr Hunter, the singing master, had the placing of this post); in the Band, also, he rose from the flute to second cornet. His cornet was an old, bashed instrument, with two moveable keys and one fixed (or stuck) key; but it did not matter, the thing could be made to play well enough so long as you did it quietly and only came in occasionally. It helped in the parts where light and shade were required. Walter, moreover, was promised a saxhorn, shortly—a long, starved-looking piece of brass, but a good loud-sounding instrument, which was always prominent in variation parts.

About this time, a number of workmen were engaged in the grounds under Dr Bedford's window, something having gone wrong with the main gas-pipe. An opening had to be made, which went straight across the gravel, from the Govie's door to the 'cond green. This turned the traffic to the east side, the west being almost always used. The operations had been very quickly performed, and not particularly well guarded.

Fuffie was coming up to his classes; he had evidently been looking in some other direction; at any rate, he disappeared down the hole about six feet deep. Luckily, he did not hurt himself; but the remark which he made several times in the hearing of the boys, "I was not aware of the circumstances and down I went," was seized upon and quoted for many a day.

One rather wild trick, although a saint would have been provoked to laugh at it, was carried on when the carts came with the coal. A little fellow, named Sandy, took a particular

204 *Walter Crighton, or Reminiscences of*

delight in watching the arrival of the necessary supplies, especially if he observed new men in charge. The carts stopped at the outside of the pend gate, and the men having the pieces of coal piled upon their backs carried them into the coal-house.

As they turned the corner, out popped Sandy with a short leather strap, and whack, whack, whack, whack would

SANDY AND THE COALMAN.

resound on the back of the man's legs to his undisguised astonishment and pain, followed by a volubility which was not on some occasions very complimentary. On coming in with the second load the man would be assailed in the same manner. His tormentor, of course, was never visible, always disappearing amongst the pillars, and dodging about until at length he hid himself at the back of the 'cond school stair, where he would sit down and smile delightedly over his trick.

In the morning, and at night before the Chapel, it was the duty of the two lads in the precentor's box to light the gas, and after the service was over to put it out again. One morning after Chapel, as Walter turned down the lights in the pulpit, he thought of gratifying a long-felt desire, namely, to climb down by the heavy carving which adorned it. Going over the right hand side he began his descent, but catching hold of a part of the ornamental work it broke off short, and he went tumbling down into one of the great armchairs. Fortunately, he was not hurt, but both he and his companion were in fear of being found out, for the large broken piece was easily noticeable. Taking it upstairs, they laid it in its place, and in the course of the day managed by heating or melting a piece of oil-silk with a match to fix it on.

CHAPTER XV.

A NEW HOUSE was being built at the top of the shed against the old city wall for the Steward, and capital sport the boys had in the evenings amongst the odd tools, &c., which were lying about. One evening they were romping as usual, some running along the batten divisions, each compartment containing about a dozen cartloads of putty lime which had been lying for two or three days. It would be some twenty inches deep, and had a nice crusty appearance on the top.

After crossing the centre batten several times they grew bolder, and a little fellow, nick-named "the pig," thought of standing for an instant in the centre. Unfortunately, he had a swinging fit, his arms going like the wings of a wind-mill. It was no use, he could not regain his balance, so in he went flat on the top of the slimy material, and disappeared.

After his chums got over their surprise, their assistance was readily given to extricate him. This was done with great difficulty, and none too soon.

When his eyes and mouth were cleared, and his figure was, as it were, blocked out, he was set upon one of the forms of the shed, and seven or eight boys busied themselves as hard as they could with small pieces of lath at modelling.

Any onlooker would have thought that extra hands were on a statuary job in a hurry. With patience, however, and by dint of careful scraping, "the pig" was made tolerably clean. The warder having noticed him, and demanded particulars, the order was given to shut the shed gate in the evenings. Further sport in that quarter was thus out of the question.

Walter, along with some half-a-dozen others, instead of sitting on Sunday with the rest of the boys in the church gallery, went downstairs to the choir. There were also a number of the Watson's Hospital boys. Unfortunately for Walter at this time (although I believe it was the means of bringing about a better feeling between the two sets of lads—the knaps and the "neets") he and one of them got to high words, and Mr King, their Governor, complained to Dr Bedford about it. Walter and Carruthers were ordered to go and see the Doctor at his house that night at six o'clock.

Punctually at the time, the two made their way up to his rooms, wondering yet fearing what he wanted to see them about. On reaching the door they knocked timidly, and one of the Doctor's servants turned them by a lobby on the left and a door on the right into a bright little room which was the Doctor's study.

When they had sat for about five minutes on one of the corners of a chair, turning their caps round and round in their hands, as if seeking to find an end to the rim of them, and feeling very uncomfortable and out of place, they heard the well-known soft step of the Doctor. He opened the door (one would think he had almost to stoop to enter), and closing it behind him he walked over to the fireplace. Putting his hands behind his back, and stretching his legs apart, he looked at the two boys for a second or two, then passing his fingers through his hair, as if he wished to remove it altogether, he began—"Well, boys, I am very sorry to have to call you here. I have just had a visit from the Governor of George Watson's Hospital about a very unpleasant occurrence —but I have no doubt you know well enough what it was he spoke to me about." (This he said with one of his peculiar smiles which it was always difficult to interpret.)

"Do you understand what I mean?" he asked.

Both boys were standing staring at the carpet, and made no answer.

The Doctor resumed: "I had vainly hoped that on the last occasion of disagreement with the Watson boys, the leniency which I then showed would have had the effect of putting a stop to any repetition of that vengeful spirit, on your part at any rate. I am extremely disappointed to have been mistaken, and I should really wish if you have anything to say for yourselves that you would say it."

After questioning them thoroughly he found that some difference about hymn-books had led to sly kicks and threats of what was in store for next Saturday.

Summing up he said: "I cannot find a loophole of excuse for you boys, and, as I was lenient before, I must now be severe. I am determined to stamp out this feeling with the utmost of my power; therefore, both of you will be confined on Saturday all day, and have a half-text copy each to fill. Now, you may go."

The two lads quitted the Doctor's study with sad hearts. They were so surprised that they never spoke a word, until they reached the terrace outside of the pend gate. The silence was broken by Carruthers.

"Do you think we'll be confined the hale day?" he asked.

"A dinna ken," replied Walter, " he certainly means it the now; maybe he'll change his mind an' make it half. A m rare gushin' about it, for a wis gaun oot tae Davidson's Mains tae see some friends o' ours wi' my mother and sisters. They'll be vexed tae, but we canna help it. A winder hoo King kent about it? The 'boukie sumph' o' a 'neet' mun hae telt him."

"I dinna think that," said Carruthers, "for I saw King watching us frae ower where he sits in the gallery, and he's a proper birsy yin."

On Saturday morning, after service in the Chapel Walter and Carruthers heard their names read out, as the Doctor had said, "all day"; and soon afterwards the two prisoners were seeing from their cell windows the bright, happy, laughing stream of boys on their way out.

Many things and times had their bright side to us boys, but this, for unalloyed delight, we think beat them all. The Saturday morning, free from all care, light of heart, the soul overflowing with anticipated pleasures, knowing that we would meet bright, cheerful welcomes from our loving friends at home, we all prepared schemes from which were got endless enjoyment and mirth. Oh, it was grand! Of course it had its other side, and that was when we came in at night. Indeed, the Saturday nights' in-comings have caused longing sighs, and tears enough to float a war vessel. As the morning was truly happy, the evening was verily miserable.

No need then to enlarge upon the longing looks that were cast by Walter and his fellow prisoner after their companions. The door was locked, and would not be opened until dinner time. It was one comfort that they were not put on bread and water.

The room in which they were confined was the writing-school. Going under the desk, which ran along in front of the east-most window, they had a good long look out, watching the soldiers drilling on the Castle Esplanade, and the "dakies" and "blackies" hopping about on the 'ird greens, of which, along with two old wickets, one standing, the other on the ground, and an old bat, they were just now the undisturbed possessors.

CONFINED IN THE WRITING-SCHOOL.

Walter turned away with a heavy sigh, and went back underneath the desk, followed by Carruthers. Seating themselves at one end of the long table, their copy-books before them, they examined the line which was to be written all over the copy. Exclusive of the top text, it was "*Shun that which is evil.*" Walter counted the leaves and quietly abstracted the two centre ones, telling Carruthers to do the same. Tearing them up, he remarked, "That makes them four pages less onyway. Now for a pin-in, and when it's done we'll tell some stories."

At it they went ; by dinner time the copies were more than half done, and when the wardsman opened the door to let them down to the hall, he found them both very busy. Kail, "touts, and cone," and a "dose" were soon partaken of, the warder waiting the while. When they had finished, they were walked back to the writing-school and locked in again. In silence they resumed work on their copies, and when the man appeared with their "chit and milk" (or tea) they had only two sides to finish. The porringers being removed, they made a quiet survey of all unlocked cupboards and presses in the room.

"Hurrah," said Walter, "see what I've found," and he held up a ball of kite twine. "We'll make use of this when the knaps come in."

Stories were told, and the time was passed amusing themselves with sundry bits of trash which they got in some of the places.

"If the Belfry wis only open," said Carruthers, "we might put off the time fine."

"Aye," said Walter, "but wishing 'll no' open that old lock." So they had to content themselves where they were. Finishing their copies, they went to the window. It was now getting grey dark, and lifting the sash they saw the knaps beginning to come straggling in.

Walter got his ball of twine, and a look about for something to let over discovered nothing to suit his purpose. However, he took off his boot, and tying one end of the cord to the top eyelets, he lowered it over the window, down,

down, until it rested on the stone runner at the side of the gravel. As one of the boys passed, Walter jerked the boot up and down until he saw that it was noticed.

The knap came forward, and putting his hand in his pocket dropped something into the boot, just as a person might drop a coin into the church plate, possibly with a more charitable feeling. Up, up they pulled it, when to their great delight they found that it contained a number of splendid "katie flips." Down went the boot again, and each time it was taken up they added to their store. Down once again to the bottom. They sat on the edge of the desk, waiting, and before long the string again commenced to wriggle. "There's a bite," said Walter, and they ran to the window to pull up. Carruthers looked out but could see no one.

"They must have bolted hanged quick into the pend gate," he remarked.

"Never mind them, it's their 'sock' we want," said Walter, and up came the boot. This time to their intense consternation and disgust it contained the *lodge tawse*.

"Crickie! here's a scrape," said Carruthers.

Walter, however, feeling wroth against "Sprat" (for it could only be he), took his knife and cut the tawse in four pieces, which he carefully dropped under the fire-place. This put a stop to the boot business, so the prisoners quietly munched their "sock," and waited to be relieved.

In a short time the key was turned, the door opened, and in stepped "Sprat-catcher," looking darkly at the lads under his black bushy eyebrows, and curling up his sneering lip. Waiting a while to give effect to what he was about to say, he at length began :

"Well, what game is this you have been up to?" Neither of them spoke.

"You are fine fellows. Where's the last sweets that came up in the boot?"

Walter held out two or three pieces of toffee.

"Come, now, it's the last ones I want."

"Well, that's the last sweets," said Walter, bravely.

"Perhaps and perhaps not. What was pulled up last? Was it not leather?"

"Yes," answered Walter.

"Then give it to me."

Walter quietly unfastened his boot, and taking it off put it in the wardsman's hand. At this Carruthers laughed, and the warder smiled in spite of himself.

"Come, now, no nonsense," he said, flinging it down. "Where is the tawse? They came up last."

"I don't know anything about them coming up," answered Walter, as he fixed his boot-lace.

"You little scoundrel, I'll have you before the Doctor to-night if you don't deliver them up immediately."

"You can have me where you like," said Walter, who after losing his day's outing felt quite indifferent about the upshot now.

Seeing he could make nothing of Crighton, the warder turned to Carruthers.

"Do you know anything about them?"

"I think they must have dropped out," said he, in a hesitating way.

"It's well for both of you if they have," muttered "Sprat"; and, addressing Walter, "As for you, I'll have my eye on you for the future."

Walter was about to make a rather pert remark as to where his eye had been in the past, but he held his tongue.

"Bring your copies and follow me to the lodge."

They followed him down, and deposited their copy-books on the table, "Sprat" looking carefully underneath the window for the lost tawse. He groped about for some time, the other two wardsmen meanwhile laughing at him and joking the boys as to which of them swallowed the strap. At last "Sprat" returned, very red and furious at being done in his own game.

"Where did you put them?" he demanded. Walter looked at the ceiling, Carruthers looked at the floor, but neither spoke.

"Aye! Come with me!" and marching the two across the square he took them straight up to the Doctor. The latter was sitting in his study, writing. "Sprat" told him how they had been wasting their time, instead of attending to their copies, and that they had denied having got the tawse. The Doctor looked annoyed and vexed; he ordered the warder to leave them to him, and "Sprat" made his exit. Looking at the boys, he asked, quietly. "Did you get many sweetmeats in this way?"

"Yes, sir," answered Walter.

"What suggested the plan to you?"

"We found a long piece of string in one of the desks."

"Yes; then you were rummaging the place instead of attending to your poena," said the Doctor, smiling. "Did you finish your task?"

"Yes, sir," both answered.

"Um! And now tell me the truth: Did you find the tawse in the boot?"

"Yes, sir," answered Walter.

"Ah! why did you tell the wardsman that you did not get them?"

"He asked if we pulled up leather and we said 'yes'—a boot: then he asked if the tawse came up, and we said 'no': and that we never heard of tawse coming up a wall."

The Doctor, who always appreciated a joke, nodded his head in assent to the logical argument, but reminded Walter that in his opinion prevarication was as bad as direct lying.

"And what did you do with them?"

"Cut them up and put the pieces at the back of the fireplace."

The Doctor simply stared at the two boys, who fully expected to be told off for next Saturday.

"Well, well, go downstairs, and I'll see to this."

They made a bow, and as quickly as possible got downstairs into the square. Ross and one or two more were waiting for them; Ross having been to Walter's home to tell his mother why he could not be out, made matters as pleasant as possible. Mrs Crighton had asked him to tell Walter that she would be at the Church door on the morrow. Walter received a good bag of "sock," sent by his sisters, accompanied with an injunction to see and not be confined next Saturday.

The winter had passed with the usual sports and games. A shift forward was made in the wards from the third to the second. The latter ward was attended to by "Sprat-catcher," who had a bed at the lower end, next to the lavatory door. It was boxed in with a partition about six feet high. The fireplace on the east side of the room was guarded by a large cage, the door of which had a padlock, although the key was seldom if ever turned in it.

On the Saturday night after "Sprat" went downstairs, the boys who had brought in mealy puddings hung them from the bars of the cage in front of the fire, where they spluttered and fizzed to their intense satisfaction—satisfaction arising not only from possession but from the "chawing" which this possession would give the others. Generally the tit-bits were fairly well-divided, although the monastic system is certainly calculated to breed selfishness, on account of always getting, and having very little to give. It was wonderful how few there were of that nature, for the "sock" &c., was always freely shared.

One of the horrors of this ward was the boot-brushing. To the general reader the question may arise—What great horror could there be in boot-brushing? Even although the reader be an auld callant, if he was not in Sprat's ward he may wonder what could be in the boot-brushing to constitute a horror.

The leather used in the making of the boys' boots was not of the very finest. It was good and strong, but until well worn, it was not calculated to take on a very brilliant polish. Say it was a Saturday night, following a rainy, muddy day. The knaps were tired and more ready for bed than anything else. After prayers each one had to don his chalker, buckle up sleeves, and repair to the washing-house. They all congregated round the long table, at either end of which was a large ball bottle, and having selected from one of the drawers as good a pair of brushes as possible, the work began. This was about half-past nine, and we have seen two or three still round that table with anger in their hearts, and tears in their eyes, rub, rub, rubbing, when the hour of midnight struck. "Sprat" seemed to take a delight in tormenting. After the wet boots were polished, at least to the satisfaction of any reasonable being, they were presented for inspection. "No," he would growl out; and back you had to go again and polish, polish, polish, very likely to be put back again half-a dozen times afterwards.

An event which always delighted the boys, as well as the parents and friends, was what was called "Gleedie's Exam." The preliminaries had been gone through, and all had shown up well; the different steps and sets were, indeed, almost perfect. A new dance had been in preparation, namely, the sword dance. It had only been given to the highest class, but Walter, having watched closely the senior boys practising in the shed during their play-hours, had picked it up very well. On the Friday, the evening on which the ball was held, each class had an hour's practice.

When the one in which Walter was had finished, Mr M'Glashan remarked that he was sorry not to have any of them able to do the sword dance at the exhibition, but it should form part of their lesson next season. At this some of the boys shouted out that Crighton could do it. "Gleedie" straightened himself up, called Walter out, and asked if such were the case.

"I don't know," was the answer, given in rather a shy manner.

"Come and we will see," and laying down a pair of laths, which were used instead of swords, he picked up his fiddle and struck up "Ghillie-Callum."

Walter got into his place, and went through the four figures without a mistake. The teacher was in high glee, and patting him on the head said he should dance to-night along with the other class. This immensely pleased Walter's chums, who really felt proud that he was going to do it.

At five o'clock two oranges were given to each boy, and after leaving the hall they dressed for the evening party.

The company gathered about six o'clock. The place where the fête was held was in the Heriot Bridge School, which now looked quite gay with all the friends of the boys sitting round. The admission was by ticket, two of which were given to each boy. The tickets had a commercial value of sixpence and fourpence respectively.

The top of the room was set with chairs, which were occupied by the Govies and their friends.

In the centre of the north side sat the string band, led by Mr Laubach. Two first violins, a cornet, and a double bass discoursed beautiful music, quite different to dance to from the music of "Gleedie's" auld fiddle. The youngest classes were being examined first, and the word for Walter's section to get ready was brought up to the "Wark." Getting in order, they marched down the shrubbery walk and through by a door into the play-ground in connection with the school.

Those who had already been put through their paces passed out, and the others went in. The bright warm room and the strange faces made it all very bewildering to the boys. The band struck up, places for quadrilles were called, and each one went to his different set. By a clap of his hands the teacher put the boys in motion, and through they went almost without a mistake. The lancers and other dances having been finished, they were passed out, and the others, the highest class, came in, the master telling Walter to stay behind.

"GLEDDIE'S EXAM.," HERIOT BRIDGE SCHOOL.

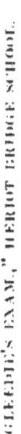

On quietness being once more obtained, one of the boys set the sticks for ten to dance the sword dance. After the ten had taken their places, Mr M'Glashan lifted another set of sticks, and calling Crighton, said, "Now, ladies and gentlemen, this is one of my best boys, and he will dance this dance which I never taught him, he having learned it from seeing the others." Laying down the sticks, he put Walter in position. The band struck up and the dancers set in motion.

Walter managed to get through the first two figures very well, but, through looking for a moment at the others, he lost his step and stood quite still. On went the dance, and a very good finish was made, the point being in the last figure. As the band quickens its time, the dancer must also quicken his step, and the one who finishes without touching his cross-swords, or is the last to touch them, is reckoned best. All, however, towards the end had sent their sticks spinning. They were loudly cheered, and the other dances were in turn proceeded with.

At the close, another trial of the sword dance was specially asked for. Mr M'Glashan approached Walter, who was sitting beside his mother and his sister Kate, with a very crest-fallen look on his face, and said, "Come, Crighton, you must try again."

Walter was rather inclined not to try, but was ultimately prevailed upon, with the advice to look after his own feet and he could not go wrong. He rose and took his place before the swords. The tittering of the other dancers only served to make him more determined. The music started, and away they went, all eyes being turned upon Walter. To the great surprise of all, two of the others went wrong through looking at Walter and not attending to themselves. On they went till the last step, and as the band quickened Walter was still as correct as ever. Quicker and quicker got the music; the dancers stopped one after another, until all were out except Walter, who finished with the band, his sticks lying as they had been laid down. Quite an ovation rewarded his change of luck, which pleased Walter very much. This finished the entertainment, and after a few remarks from some of the Govies, the boys went back to the "Wark," and the visitors retired, pleased with the excellent exhibition they had seen.

CHAPTER XVI.

THE next day was of course a holiday. With a large number of knaps the usual way of spending it was by disporting themselves in the Swimming Baths at Pitt Street. By 11 o'clock, a good number had gathered in the Baths, and what between swimming, diving, swinging in the boat which hung across the pond, and the large revolving cage at the shallow end, climbing the different ropes, enjoying themselves sitting on the long, zinc, hot seat up in the gallery, and eating Threipland's currant "bricks," a good day's fun was had. The currant "bricks" were something terrible — grand, heavenly! If you ate a few of them they would keep your stomach for a week. Then there was the trapeze. Tommy Mice went on them with his clothes on, and had to be hung up to dry—he stuck in the middle and had to drop in, clothes and all. Across the tube, diving from the spring boards, &c., &c.—in fact, a splendid day's fun was always had in the Baths after "Gleedie's Exam."

On the next Friday evening a very interesting Lecture was given by the two German captives who were liberated by the British from King Theodore of Abyssinia; the curious manner in which they told their story being cleverly imitated by some of the knaps for many a day after, to the delight of the different parlour groups who gathered to hear them.

Walter's class had just entered the writing-school one morning, and "Nibbie" was a little behind his time in arriving. One of the boys jumped up with the remark, "What do you say tae bar 'Nibbie' out?"

This was something new: at least it had not been tried for sometime.

"All right," came from every side. Forms, chairs, &c., were piled up against the door, and the footfall of the master was anxiously listened for. There was not long to wait.

"There he is," came from half-a-dozen knaps.

"A' sit quiet," was the order given by one of the elder boys. Up came "Nibbie," and on reaching the door turned the handle, all to no purpose. Push, push, push, and a grumbling and talking reached the ears of the lads. He had evidently discovered that the door was not locked, as it had given way a little, and "Nibbie" knew enough to be aware of what was behind.

"Open that door," he shouted. No one answered. Again came the order, but still no response.

"I know what you scoundrels are after, and if that door is not opened at once I'll go for the Doctor." He was now belabouring the door with the handle of his umbrella. The elder boys were sitting trying to smother their laughter as best they could, stuffing handkerchiefs into their mouths; some of the young ones being rather terrified at the whole affair.

"Nibbie" evidently saw that the boys were not going to be bullied, so he now tried coaxing. "Come now, lads, open the door, and I'll say no more about it; I'm sure you've all had enough of fun now."

This only brought a burst of laughter, which had the effect of again raising his ire. He pushed once more with might and main at the door, but could not move it, for besides having a load of furniture to shift, the forms and all available corners were weighted with boys.

"I'll just give you one more chance," came from the outside, which, however, did not make the knaps budge an inch. "Well, here goes for the Doctor," and pacing out of the lobby "Nibbie" went down the stair. The boys were "cleeking" from the windows which looked into the square, and as he did not pass over they calculated that he had not carried out his threat. After a lapse of about five minutes his step was again heard approaching. Turning the door handle he made one more trial, but the barricade was still there. Finding it was no use he went downstairs again, this time furiously determined to go for the Governor.

The boys waited until they saw the two gentlemen passing the "connie" windows in the Govie's stair. Pulling back the forms and setting everything square, they all got in order and into their seats. "Nibbie" tried the door with a push which brought him into the room rather more quickly and forcibly than he expected, to the very evident amusement of the boys. The Doctor was serious. The twelve eldest boys were called out and had "half-a-dozen" each; but, judging from after conversation of the boys, the joke was well worth the punishment.

"What's up wi' the 'Wee Buck,' that he's been sittin' in the parlours these three days?"

The question was asked by one of the lads at Walter.

"Oh," was the answer, "he's been 'maukin' tae get off wi' Nipper's class, an' he says he's no gaun tae Bob's aither.

He swears it's the toothache. You should hae seen him heating his hanky at the fire and rubbing his jaw tae make it red."

Bob's class met in the Museum, and he had evidently been missing the "Wee Buck." Glancing round the class, he asked quietly, "Is there any boy absent?" No answer.

"Where is White?"

"He's got the toothache," ventured half-a-dozen at once.

"Yes; and is he in the sickroom?"

The boys hesitated. That was enough for Bob; he knew the lads well enough by this time, and was well aware from the hesitation that all was not right. Singling out one, he questioned him and found that White was not in the sickroom but in the parlours.

"Aye! Very well, go down and tell him I wish to see him."

The boy retired and in a few minutes returned with the "Wee Buck" behind him. The invalid's face was very red, and bore signs of furious rubbing. The other lad took his seat, leaving White standing in the middle of the floor, apparently very interested between the toe of his boot and the contents of the cases ranged round the walls. Bob gave him plenty of time to think the matter over.

At last he said, "Well, White, the boys tell me you are very ill with the toothache; is that so?"

"Yes, sir."

"Poor fellow; has it been very severe?" (This compassionately.)

"Yes, sir, very." Here the "Wee Buck" nodded with energy, putting his hand to his face as if the very question had caused a sudden twinge of excessive pain

"Yes; and have you seen the nurse?" asked Bob, very feelingly.

"Yes, sir."

Of course this was true enough. Meenie could be made to swallow the toothache easily enough at any time.

"And what did she order you to do for it?"

"Nothing for it, sir, but heat and rest."

"Oh yes, dear me," said Bob.

"Have you been to the dentist?"

"No, sir," answered White.

"What! you've had the toothache three days, and not been to have the tooth pulled out? What nonsense; come and let me see it; I sometimes can do a little for *your* kind of toothache." This he said still assuming a sympathising manner.

White opened his mouth, but very unfortunately had not made up his mind as to the particular tooth which was giving him pain. Fixing on one which was perfectly good and sound, he pointed to it as the one. The master could not see why it should cause him pain; however, he would do something for it, which he was sure would entirely take all the nasty feeling away, as it made heat; then he could sit down and rest. Going to his drawer he took out his tawse and administered as sound a dozen as ever he gave either before or after. Strange to say, White was completely cured, and also all would-be "maukers"— in Bob's class at anyrate!

A number of boys, including Walter, Ross, Johnstone, Sinclair, Tod, Kidd, and a few more were going to jump the wall into Greyfriars to fetch a "find" discovered by one of their number.

In one of his rambles amongst the old tombs, Sinclair had come across a skull and some old bones which he had hid behind a corner of a low dyke, at a place not easy of access to the ordinary visitor. They met at the connie of the seventh green, and watching their opportunity were soon on the other side of the dyke, where they held a council round Anderson's tomb as to further movements. Their arrangements duly made, they got over the railings and up by the right. At the top of the walk they turned to the left, and went straight into the main portion of the churchyard.

"I say, Ross," whispered Walter, "I think we are gey like the resurrectionists that ran away wi' 'Puddin'' an' drapt him in the Candlemaker Row."

After they had got over the rising ground they felt easier, and interested themselves looking at the quaint old memorial stones. Arriving at the bottom or north side of the ground, Sinclair went across a barrier, and reaching his hand over a little dyke, he drew up the skull and laid it on the grass, staring with its large sightless eye-holes at the cluster of wondering boys. Walter really felt rather a curious sensation pass over him as he thought that perhaps the former owner of that row of still shining teeth and shapely forehead might be watching the present operations (but of course it did not matter much as the skull was joint property now). Johnstone diving his hand over again brought up a handful of bones, which he passed out to his companions. Then they all took a short cut over the grass, but they had not gone many yards when a cry from one of their number brought them to a sudden stop. He was standing with his hands up, staring, and with a look of either surprise or terror on his countenance, his eyes starting out of his head, mouth open, rooted to the spot on which he stood.

"What's the matter, Kidd?" they all gasped out at once.

"Oh, what's that?" They clustered round the spot, and Mackay turned over with his foot what proved to be a dead duck!

"Ah," said Ross, "that wid make a rare prap." No sooner said than done; back went the duck, which was stuck on a spike of the high railings, each one taking a handful of the largest pebbles which the gravel afforded. Walking a short distance back, they commenced "firing shots," each one after passing the duck and going over the wall making a rattling sound as if it had been aimed at a conservatory for a target.

However, every boy had to finish his collection of stones, no matter where they went. A stir on the other side of the wall made them take to their heels and make for the "Wark." There they arrived all right with their treasure, which they deposited in one of the gutter traps at the front of the 'ird green stairs, to be more minutely examined on the morrow.

All went to their different rooms for preparation, and after the Hall to Chapel. Prayers were over, and the Doctor stood in front of the "box" in which Walter was sitting. He signalled to the boy who opened the door to let it remain closed. After a pause he remarked that a number of the boys had been seen in the churchyard stone-throwing. Nearly every pane of glass in a large window of a school in the vicinity had been broken.

"I'm sure," he continued, "it is very painful to me that complaints of this kind are constantly coming in. I know very well that boys will be boys, but really this is overstepping the mark. I will call upon all those who were in the company to stay behind, and, besides that they will be punished themselves, their parents will have to pay for the damage done." The doors were opened, and the boys marching out left our friends still seated. After a good stiff lecture, they were taken over to the lodge and the Doctor delivered a castigation with more energy than was usual, each also having to pay a sum on the Saturday. On reaching the ward the story was told, which led to the recital of many others.

"What's that story about?" asked Tyndal. "The knaps gaun up for nests? I've heard you telling it to Tait."

"Oh, that's about the blind knap," said Grant.

"Aye," said Tyndal.

Then Grant began: "It happened in this ward we're in the now. They used to keep doos in the connie barty turrets, and often the knaps wid gang up and herrie the dookits. There was yin, an awfu' short-sighted sowl, an' no' that he wis fud, but he would never gang out wi' them, so yae nicht they codded him on tae gang, and at last he promised. They a' went doun to yon windie (pointing to the north-west corner), and three or four got oot on tae the leads, and pu'd him up after them. They crawled up tae the barty, and got their skull caps fu' o' eggs (they were a' in their chalkers, only the skull caps for tae carry the eggs). When they came doun tae the windie they a' got in but the strongest knap and this buckin' yin. They that went doun had made it up that this strong yin was tae let him doun ower the tap o' the windie, and when they had a hud o' him below they were tae say 'A' richt,' and the strong knap was tae let go. Everything went well enough until, just as the knaps inside o' the windie said 'A' richt,' somebody cried '*sel*,'' and they a' bolted tae their beds, an' the blinkin' knap disappeared athegither ower the windie.

"The strong yin on the tap didna ken but that everything was richt enough until he came in, and a rare fricht they a' got, but never said onything, an' went tae their beds.

"In the morning when the cook went out tae feed her hens, as she opened the door (in the dyke that ran between the kitchen connie and the shed wall at that time) there was the knap sittin' wi' his knees up at his chin, an' looking terribly cauld. After asking him what he was sittin' there for, she got an awfu' fricht; *he was stane deid*. It wis fund oot that he had crawled aboot after he fell, an' if they had only gien the alarm at the time, he micht have been saved."

One of the lads then proposed—"If you like I'll read you a story that I fund in an auld book; it's aboot an auld knap—yin o' the garriers." All assented, and when they were silent he proceeded to read as follows:

"James Hay, the son of a stabler in the Grassmarket, was arrested for petty theft from a Canongate dram-shop, and as at that time this crime was punishable with hanging, he was ordered to be executed. On the evening before the execution, his father visited him in the old Tolbooth Prison. He took some liquor with him, and invited the jailer to partake of it. The jailer did so, and in a short time was rather tipsy. The old man plied him liberally, and being allowed to have some conversation with his son, gave him some hurried instructions.

"When the closing hour came, old Hay suggested that as this was the last night his boy had on earth, the warder might allow him to remain a little longer, and also if he would get some more rum, they might have another dram. The now tipsy keeper agreed, and proposed to go and get the liquor himself. Hay gave him some money and downstairs he stottered, young Hay closely following. The turnkey opened the outer door for the warder, then closed it again. The boy crouched in a dark corner and waited. Before the warder had time to return, the father, putting out his head from one of the windows over the gate, cried out 'Turn your hand,' which was the House signal when any of the officials desired admittance. The turnkey at once opened the door, and no one being there he took a pace or two outside.

"Now was Hay's chance; with a bound he rushed past, was outside and away before the astonished turnkey had time to think of what had occurred. In a few minutes the High Street was in a scene of uproar, and the Watch was called out. Away sped Hay down through Beith's Wynd like an arrow from a bow, never pausing until he reached the Cowgatehead. All breathless he arrived at the lower end of the Greyfriars Churchyard wall, near to the Grassmarket, where one of his fellow apprentices met him. They exchanged no words, but the boy slipped a parcel into his hands, and then bending his back Hay put his foot on the lad's shoulder, and up, up gradually until he got hold of the top of the dyke, when with a strong pull and a lurch he was over into the churchyard.

"All this was done quickly and quietly, and when the night watchmen and officers of the guard were scouring the vicinity, the friendly apprentice boy was sauntering slowly up the Candlemaker Row, whistling a quaint tune, and a perfect picture of innocence.

"But to follow the condemned lad: Landing on the grass, he crouched down, breathing hard and listening to the hurrying and word-passing which was going on in the street. The oaths themselves were enough to frighten any ordinary person, and the imprecations of the disappointed jailers were fearful to listen to.

"As soon as he saw the lights turned out in the surrounding houses, and had quietness once more, he made a rapid move across to the north-end and passed quickly to the west wall. Creeping up past Bannatyne's, Byres', and Cunningham's tombs, right up to the corner at the Martyrs' Prison, he took a breathing space of a few minutes and a hurried glance of his surroundings.

"Oh, what agony he was suffering—a timid lad whose constitution had been much shaken, the result of a serious illness in his youth. He felt as if both his mental and physical strength were leaving him. Again onward, this time along the south wall, on to his goal, on to where he should find rest. And what a place to rest in—Heaven help him! He crept on until he reached the door of Mackenzie's Mausoleum. Here he paused, and seating himself on the steps, weary and heartless, he wept.

"The door was locked, but remembering his father's injunctions, he opened the parcel which he had received from the boy. In it was a false key, a tinder box and steel, and a bunch of candles. Rising to his feet, he opened the stout oaken door, but with a start he paused on the threshold, suddenly remembering that as a wee laddie, he had many times cried in through the keyhole—

    "'Bluidy Mackenzie! come out if you daur,
    Lift the sneck and draw the bar—'

and then scampered away as fast as he could. Now, good God! he had to pass in through that very door.

"Once on the inside and the door closed and locked, his sight tried to pierce the black darkness, but he could discern nothing, and in his imagination he was beginning to see long claw-like fingers, and hollow glaring eyes peeping at him from every corner.

"Taking his tinder-box he soon had a light, and looked for a corner in which to hide. Anyone coming into the place would see him at once, for there was nothing but the bare walls, and the stone-flags on the floor. He was in an empty dungeon. Ah! here at the right hand was a thick single iron bar covering a narrow aperture leading to a vault below. Being at a circular part of the wall, he found that he could pass himself over at the centre of it. Squeezing through, his feet caught on the corner of some stones; quietly he crept down some half-dozen steps, keeping his feeble light well in front of him.

"The vault was roomy and had a musty feeling and a sickening stench. A strange feeling passed over him, and falling on the lowest steps his overstrung nerves gave way and he fainted.

"On recovering, awful thoughts passed through his mind. Where was he? What had happened? Had he been hanged and buried? Putting out his hand, it rested on the edge of a coffin. 'Ugh!' Slowly he gathered his scattered senses. Great Heavens! this was worse than death. What should he do? Where should he creep to? At every turn his hands touched a coffin. Something must be done.

"At this moment his hands fell upon the tinder-box, and nervously he lit another candle. Looking round he saw a vacant corner under the stone stair; so creeping into it he put out his light, and fell into a sound sleep.

"On awakening he felt a little refreshed, and again obtaining a light, crept upstairs, over the iron bar and into the tomb above. The daylight was streaming through the small windows placed high in the roof of the building, so that he knew it must be well on for mid-day. Hearing voices and footsteps approaching, he quickly crawled downstairs again.

"Getting a little more used to the weirdness of his position, he looked about him. There were nine or ten coffins. One was very large in size; it must either contain two, or, if one, a very large body. Several of the others were piled each on the top of its neighbour. One, evidently, had not been very long there; all fresh and new, it stood upon tressels. In a niche of the wall was a little one, easily seen to be a child's. Horror! the lids on some of them were loose.

"In turning round quickly he pressed against the large one; with a clatter the coom fell to the ground, and two staring mummy-like figures met his view. His heart gave a great leap as he saw both sit upright. They pointed their long, bony fingers at him, and then a hollow voice said, slowly, 'Flee not from Justice.' All seemed to be in motion; the lids sliding off and the bodies raising themselves, while a voice chanted from the corner:

> "'So falls our glory with one fatal blow,
> Gone is the head which did us justice show,
> That tongue from which such well-tuned words did come,
> And charmed us all, is now for ever dumb.'

"A most sepulchral voice then asked, 'Have you come to bide with us, and taint the atmosphere of our last long resting-place with the breath of a mortal of bad and evil repute, e'en an unhung criminal, fleeing from your sentence? Be it just or unjust, return from whence you came; return and pay the penalty of the law.'

"A loud knocking overhead brought him to his senses. Hunger and terror working in him made him unconscious a second time. Another knock and a peculiar whistle, which he knew well, came from overhead. He crept upstairs. Again the whistle, and a knock at the door. Remembering what his father had told him about the signal, he paused, listening for the third whistle. Then he replied with two knocks on the inside of the door.

"On this a voice cried through the keyhole, 'Is that you, Hay'?

"'Aye.'

"'Jist open the door a wee bit.'

"This done, a leather skull-cap was pushed in containing food and a large knife. Quickly he closed the door; there was a soft foot-fall, then darkness and silence reigned once more. On reaching the corner under the stairs he lighted his candle, and with a convulsive movement grasped the huge knife, holding it in front of him as if to defy the dead all around.

"After eating a portion of the food, and taking a draught from a flask of milk, he felt stronger.

"That night he slept better, and his dreams were of green country lanes, with fresh balmy air, where he was as free as the birds singing in the trees, and with his laughing happy companions was gathering the green birk for the buskin'. Oh, how sweet the breath of heaven was to him at this moment. But what an awakening!

"Next morning he lit his candle and had a look round. The horror of the place had in a sense nearly worn away, and fear of the ghastly surroundings partly left him.

"On each coffin there was a heavy brass plate, bearing the name, age, and date of death of the occupant. Great personages they were. They came down from the distant past; some had been there a hundred years and more. The screw-nails which had kept the lids in their places were rusted away, and each could be lifted off.

"In trying to shift one of the coffins, it all fell to pieces; old rotten wood, bones, and dust, tumbling down together in a heap. Reverently he collected the bones and placed them in a corner. Taking his knife he undid the screws in the new coffin and lifted the lid. The remains were those of a beautiful lady, very tall she must have been, lying as if in a sound sleep, with her right cheek resting on a pretty pillow, and swathed in pure white linen. Long he thought on her pure, peaceful rest compared with his own miserable, tired, and haunted existence. After screwing down the lid again, he felt as if he were not so terribly alone. At night the signals were repeated and food was brought.

"So the days went on for fully three weeks. At the end of that time he made the first sally outside of his prison home.

"It was midnight, and he quietly undid the door and slipped out. What glorious sniffs he took of the cool night air! how refreshing and precious they were. He dared not venture far, but he got the length of the Martyrs' Prison.

"As he brushed past a bush some little birds were startled and flew out with a whirr. Poor Hay! he was nearly frightened out of his remaining wits, and as quickly as possible returned to his dismal den.

"Two weeks and three days more he remained, then bade farewell to his fearsome domicile. Creeping down through the churchyard to the spot where he got in, he crossed over the wall and made his way down to the Grassmarket.

"At the carriers' quarters was a cart laden with empty herring barrels for shipment at Leith. Into one of the casks he stowed himself, and next morning was carted through the city gates.

"On reaching the docks he was stowed in the hold of the good ship 'Raven.' A few days afterwards they reached Rotterdam, and in time a passage to New York was secured; from there he went to Sydney.

"Now, as he rides over his wide flourishing acres in far off Australia, his thoughts sometimes go back with a shudder to the weeks spent in that awful Tolbooth prison, and still more awful and terrible sanctuary.

"The news in time reached Edinburgh, and the account now given is from a long letter sent to a friend many years after." *—So the story ended.

The merry month of June was fast approaching, and great preparations were going on, for the boys, with the help of the wardsmen, intended to make the decorations of the wards something special. Last June they had had a few coloured paper chains, &c., hung about the walls, and the novelty was thought so much of that this year a great effort was to be made in a similar direction. There would

---

* A reward of twenty guineas had been offered for the apprehension of the fugitive, or for any information which would lead to it.

be a keen competition between the fifth and the second wards; for each of the wardsmen, "Sprat" and "Ja-ra-pa," were clever fellows who, besides, spared neither pains nor money towards the success of the dormitory "buskin'."

Several of the knaps were smart at the pencil and brush, and the different shields connected with the "blue blanket" were tastefully reproduced. Large sheets of cardboard,

WARD DECORATIONS.

some hollow and others round on the surface, were made into shields, which, with their grounds of blue and bars of gold, and red and yellow stars, hammers and various devices, were fixed round the walls. The upper or south end of the ward was done up something after the manner of the decorations in the square.

Chains of coloured paper were looped over and round the shields, and crossed and re-crossed the ward, until overhead appeared to be a perfect maze of tastefully arranged and beautifully sweeping lines. Bannerettes and flags were fixed with much effect on every available point. One really wonderful specimen of boys' work occupied the centre, taking as it were the position of George Heriot's statue. This was the shield of the Heriot Arms. On a ground of gold was the bar and three roses, perhaps with too natural an appearance to please the heraldic critic. On the lower half was the five-pointed star; hanging scrolls at the sides and branching thistles on the top were crowned by an artistically-coloured helmet of steel-tints, having for a crest a little cornucopia of really genuine artistic merit.

On the evening and the night preceding June Day, they were all very busy, and everything was finished about two o'clock in the morning. During the day the wards were open to the public, and great admiration was expressed by all the visitors.

CHAPTER XVII.

THE next event which occupied much of the thoughts, the conversation, and the leisure of the knaps, was the Excursion. This year it was to be to North Berwick, and an extra good cricket match was arranged for. The parties who looked after this part of the excursion programme thought it would be useless for the boys to play the match as the only team who could play them were so much older. In fact, their club was mostly composed of young men, and was locally in high repute. However, the knaps were quite eager to give them some of the famed Heriot mixture (slow under-hand bowling) which was very deadly to players who only practised against swift round-hand. The match was kept on the card of arrangements, and the first eleven went hard at practice.

It was a good eleven, and was well captained by a lad named Wight, who knew how to work his men. Wight was, without question, the best all-round player, and also the Garr. He was one of the genuine stamp of Garrs, a regular good fellow, who could be approached by the little fellows at any time with their complaints.

Others of the team were good batsmen. One in particular, named Glass, was a terrible "swiper"; it was nothing for him to send a ball from the pitch in the seventh green through the glass of the parlour window, and that was a good "on drive." Then, one of the bowlers delivered the most coaxing "mixtures" it was possible to give.

A new set of wickets, and two prime 16 cane-handled bats had been bought at Percy King's in Lothian Street. They had got a great bargain of them—guinea bats for ten shillings, and they were stunners. There were also two brand-new, red match balls, new pads and wicket gloves. With all this, and with "Billy" to coach them, it was a case of "Come on, M'Duff."

On the morning of the Excursion, after an early breakfast and the usual performance of examining baskets, &c., they were soon being whisked on to North Berwick.

On arriving there, they encamped on a fine grassy bank facing the sea. "Baps and lamb" were doled out, and then a party proceeded under the care of Levick to have a bathe.

A local function had been arranged for that day in connection with the launch of the life-boat, and the "Wark" band was requested to supply the music. Both governors and boys readily complied, and the band playing a lively march proceeded up the town to where the car with boat and crew on it was stationed. A procession was then formed which, after traversing some of the principal streets, arrived at the shore, where to the strains of "The Boatie Rows"—and the "Wark" band could just play "The Boatie Rows" with a vengeance—the gallant craft shot into the bay. It was great fun for the knaps to witness the capsizing of the boat, and a lusty cheer came from them as she rose like a duck on the water. The crew all scrambled in again, with the exception of one who swam ashore to show the usefulness of his cork life-belt.

After dinner, all who intended to see the cricket match were told to follow, as the eleven were going to the ground which was a short way out of the town. It was a splendid pitch, only that the "swipers" had not much chance of giving the ball "heels," as the land sloped gently upwards on either side ; the only "go" was a straight drive seawards. A lucky six might be had in that direction, but hitting either to "leg" or "off" was only for a four, and it would have to be well run to get four for it. The next speculation was the opposing team.

If age, weight, and flannels make a cricketer, then it was a bad look-out for the knaps this time. The captain was a whiskered man of about thirty years of age, clad in a white flannel knicker-bocker suit. The rest were much alike, but the captain alone wore the knickers, and whiskers, and so was at once unanimously nicknamed "Spindle-shanks." "Billy," acting as usual as umpire and general guide for the boys, won the toss, putting the knaps first to bat.

The North Berwick men were clever fielders, and runs were scarce and slow. The bowling was round hand and very swift, but the "dorers" of the "Wark" eleven managed to run up a score of 57, only one "six" being gained by a lost ball which went amongst the shingle on the beach.

After all were out, extras and everything counted, they had a score of 63. The North Berwick men were surprised at the boys, as they called them, gaining so many runs, but they were confident of success, nevertheless.

Alas ! they had never tried to digest any of the peculiar Heriot "mixtures."

In high glee, "Spindle-shanks" went first in front of the "stumps," placing himself in a fancy attitude much to the delight of the knaps. The first ball of course was the trial. A nice, swift, under-hand "lob" was delivered. This he lifted nearly as high as Berwick Law, smiling the while to his companions as much as to say—"that is only a foretaste of what I am going to give them."

The little bowler, after receiving the ball, gave it two turns between his palms and carefully measured his four steps for a run. Facing round, and coming gently up he sent in a nice, slow, long-pitched twister—temptation itself. It was too much for "Spindle-shanks," whose mighty swing was only half-an-inch too short, and the next instant the bails rolled quietly from his wickets. He seemed bewildered, and so did his companions, who depended on him for a scorer and fully expected that he would carry his bat.

His disappointment was, indeed, very marked. As he came into the camp he flung down his bat, utterly dejected and crestfallen. However, better luck was expected for the next man. He was also led into a mistake by being too greedy, and nearly every one made the same error. They seemed to loose all caution; some of the latter players being determined to run in were quickly removed by Wight, who was behind the pads.

When the cry of "all out" was given, the total was found to be 16 runs, 3 overthrows, and 2 no-balls, making a grand total of 21. The knaps made an offer to put them in again which was not accepted.

Several of the masters and the Doctor were waiting at the rendezvous to hear the result. Dr Bedford smiled in his usual way when he was informed of the win, proud, as he always was, of the success of his boys. After a few races and games (if the place was suitable), which generally wound up the day, preparations were made for the return journey.

Great fun was got from an altercation which arose between two of the masters. If they had been drinking milk with the boys we should have blamed that, but we can swear they never touched it. One master ordered the boys to go on, the other ordered them to halt; in fact, their orders were very mixed, and high words passing between the pair, the boys did not know whom to obey. Some marched, others intentionally stood still just to make matters more ludicrous. The opportunity for a muddle was, in fact, too much for the boys, and a fine muddle it was before many minutes.

Dr Bedford coming forward soon put matters right, and presently all were safe in the carriages for Edinburgh.

On the road home, the Band compartment if not a harmonious was at least a musical and extremely noisy one. Occasionally, when the "white vests" (Band Boys) could get their own instruments, a good tune would be gone through. There was no big drum on this occasion, Levick's request being that the drummer should deposit the big drum in the guard's van and use a small one. Perhaps he was afraid of his bursting the carriage; for the "Wark" big drummer either had no idea of, or would not agree to, a pianissimo in music, his ambition being to show that he had a stout stick and a willing arm.

The "Wark" was reached in safety, all being highly pleased with the day's fun and the handsome victory.

"July squeakers," "February bawsers" was now the cry, as the idea of leaving was beginning to be realised by the lawds who were about to be sent out into the wide world. After this event. Walter would be a lawd.

> "The next, a lawd in sovereign power,
> Could sway his kingly sceptre ower ;
> Tae look twad mak his highness lower,
> Then cam the order—
> Out o' your greens and schools.
> An' no come ower that border."

A lawd ! It was a magic name to every knap, and how his breast swelled out as he entered the square for the first time with the great L after his name. How he cast his glances around him, looking for some petty depredator on whom to try his power, only to see how it would work ; just as any boy might test a new pocket knife on his grandfather's walking stick to find out if the knife's edge was keen. And how closely and sharply he would watch from his lofty height for contravention on the part of the culprit.

If he should disobey, the lawd's power and importance was assailed, and then he would not miss him (even should he be a better fighter than himself).

If his first test conducted himself properly as a criminal, more than likely he would simmer down into a quiet inoffensive lawd for the rest of his term.

One great grief to Walter was the loss of his friend, Ross. He had had his turn as a lawd, and had just been the same kindly fellow. He was leaving with nothing eminently hopeful in view, but he had a good constitution, a happy spirit, and a fair education with which to begin some useful apprenticeship. A compact was made between him and Walter to meet every Saturday, so that there was still an atom of comfort left.

When the next term began, a new arrangement was to be made. Some of the boys were to become "non-residents" or day scholars; others whose parents requested it could have the liberty of staying at home over the Sunday, returning to the Hospital at eight o'clock on Monday morning. The latter arrangement had been already in vogue for some months, and a number of the boys who had availed themselves of it had applied for enrolment as non-residents.

Between twenty and thirty had received the liberty, and as several would be elected on the same terms at every election, the number would soon bring down the list of indoor boys.

The examination past, and the holidays once more fairly started, Walter was to have a week extra at home, as this would be his last summer holidays in the "Wark."

His eldest sister had left school and gone to service, so that Mrs Crighton was now in a better position to entertain her boy for a little longer, and with more comfort and less inconvenience than formerly.

The "Vacance" was much the same as formerly to those who remained in: an hour's lessons in the forenoon and the remainder of the day for romping. They were accommodated in the second ward at night; and had the usual stories and gambols. The Saturdays and Wednesdays were spent at home. Everything was done by the Governors and teachers to make the time pass pleasantly.

One or two of the Watson boys had been invited to come over and have a game at cricket, which they did along with a lad from an institution in the Portobello district. A better feeling was springing up between the knaps and "neets," which Dr Bedford did all in his power to encourage. The result of the friendly match ended in a draw.

One afternoon a number of the boys took it into their heads to pay a stolen visit to Leith. They had still the same desire to "skirt," even although they were so often out; perhaps too much spare time and less vigilant watchers had to do with this. By good luck, more than anything else, Walter was not in this batch of runaways (he had been sent out on a message for Dr Bedford), as the trip led to rather serious consequences.

The excursionists, to the number of nine or thereby, left by Heriot Bridge dykes, and made their way down to Leith, where they wandered about the docks and examined the ships to their hearts' content.

When on their way home, one of them took a curious turn of inquiry as to the working of a small winch on board one of the boats. It was standing at the side, and had evidently been used for lifting cargo out of the vessel. The lad went on deck, and while handling it the machinery somehow made a run and the little finger of his left hand getting between the tooth and pinion wheels was neatly nipped off, and fell into a watery grave. His yells and the consternation of his companions soon gathered a crowd. A cab was procured, and he was taken to Leith Hospital, where the injured hand was attended to. The now sorrowful boys made their way back to the "Wark," leaving their maimed comrade behind.

As they bolted up the shrubbery they were met by Walter and some of the others in the greens. The knaps' faces were almost as long as the walk they had just traversed; and none of them seemed able to tell or explain what had happened. After they did manage to get out the news, it became a question for discussion — What was to be done? To whom should they tell it first? It was really much too serious to think about, but after a consultation it was deemed advisable to commit themselves to Robertson, the steward. To him they accordingly went at once with the story.

Robertson immediately had a cab procured, and driving right off to Leith Hospital, he brought up the boy.

By this time the latter had come round a little, and the doctors thought he might safely undertake the journey.

Arrived at the "Wark," he was taken to the sickroom where he passed a restless night. After prayers in the Chapel, a serious lecture was delivered by "Ebbie" who was on duty; and in the lodge a still more violent and to the boys painful argument was used and feelingly taken. To this was added confinement and a diet of bread and water for a week, at which not one of the culprits grumbled, so much remorse did they feel for what had happened.

The invalid progressed favourably, and was soon downstairs. He was quite cheerful, and seemed to treat the whole affair as a clever joke rather than otherwise. He had a practice of putting his entire hand in his mouth, it having a great capacity, and, as one little fellow remarked, "it would now be easier for him to do that onyway;" to which observation the lad made answer by thrusting in not only his hand, but a worsted glove and stuffed finger as thick as a thumb, to show that his gaping power was as great as ever.

The boys had a very nice trip to Aberdour, and were taken once or twice to "Portie" to bathe before Walter left for his three weeks at home.

While out, he and two others—one a knap, nicknamed "Nanny," from his wonderful ability to bleat like a goat, and a boy who was not a Herioter—when strolling one evening along College Street were accosted by a man with rather a seafaring appearance.

A "Tar" or a "Swad" had always a special interest for the knaps. This man asked them in the nasal manner peculiar to seamen if they could put him on the right road to Leith. The lads very willingly directed him. He said, however, that being a stranger he would take it "mighty kind" if they would show him part of the way. They readily consented, it being on their own road at anyrate. Going down the Bridges, the Tar began talking and spinning yarns of sunny Spain, from whence he had just come and whither he was next bound.

When they had reached the top of Leith Walk, the boys told him that his road was now direct, and that he could not possibly miss it. Before parting, the lads promised to pay him a visit next day. He had thrown out as a bait that they should have some real delicious wine and good cigars; only they were not to be later than two o'clock, as he intended to be out of the vessel on business, and he would not like them to call in his absence. He was first mate on the "Don Juan," which was the vessel they were to look for; she was lying in the Victoria Dock, and was blue-painted to the water line. "But, remember," was his last injunction, "don't be after two."

"All right," said the boys, as they shook hands and parted. They went on, gaily talking about to-morrow's treat; and if wishes could have done it the morrow would have arrived at once. Next forenoon they met, and to put off the time they paid a visit to the Museum. Unfortunately, they stayed too long there; it was a quarter past two when they passed Pilrig clock. Hurrying down as best they could, grumbling all the way at their own stupidity, they reached the gate of the Victoria Dock at a quarter to three. They went at once to the place directed but no blue-painted vessel could they see.

They wandered round the dock but still no such vessel was to be discovered. At last they went to the officer at the gate, who informed them that such a schooner had left her moorings and been towed out not above half-an-hour ago. They told the man their story, but he only remarked, smilingly, that it was a good job they had been late. The trio could not see it; and, in fact, they were sorely disappointed. To make up for it, and that they might not exactly have had the walk for nothing, they took a dip in the sea at the Marine Parade, and then turned homewards.

On returning to the "Wark" after the holidays, Walter was entered in the first, or govies' ward, as it was called, where the outgoing boys or lawds slept. It was on the first floor of the west side, and the beds and other accommodation were much about the same as the others. To enter, you passed through a little lobby opposite the second school door, in which was one of the wifie's rooms—the room where Fummie reigned. That wifie had been a good friend to Walter. Fummie visited in the same locality as Mrs Crighton lived, and on the Monday mornings, if the wifie had been out on the previous evening, she would hand Walter a little packet of "sock" sent him by his mother.

Fummie, however, left, and another wifie, nicknamed "Big Saum'l," was put in her place. She had also a sister in the "Wark," known from her smaller size as "Wee Saum'l." Other two sisters were called respectively "Big Sodger" and "Wee Sodger." Then there was "The Baker," she having been seen to walk out with a young man who followed after that calling. Another was of dark complexion and raven locks, and was called "Blackie" accordingly. Generally speaking, the knaps did not know any other names which those damsels might possess. "Big Saum'l" was a terror in a small way; but still a soul of good nature. The knaps often tormented her, by knocking at the door and then running away; or they would fix a broom handle crossways in the dark part of the lobby, and, coaxing her to give chase, she would dive over the obstruction and measure her length in the passage. If caught, woe-betide the culprit, for "Saum'l" had an arm the biceps of which were like a lady's waist, and she could lay it on in a healthy manner.

The ward was a long room containing eighteen beds, with an enclosed bed at the north-west corner for the wardsman. At one end of the ward was the lavatory, &c., in it a long dresser with the bottles and brushes for boot-brushing. Some rare fun went on in this flat at night, and good old tales were often told. One lad, called "The Puddock," was a most humorous fellow; he was, indeed, the fountain of all sorts of "lark."

One night the knaps were rather noisy. They had a concert on, each one singing a verse to which the others could "chorus." The door opened, and "Saum'l" popped in her head with the remark that if the noise was not stopped she would report them. This was greeted with cheers and laughter, and pressing invitations to come in and sing a verse, "Cheer up, Sam," being suggested as appropriate.

This only served to irritate her, and she banged the door, swearing that—no, that's wrong: she did not swear. Let the "Wark" be a place where trickery, mimicry and devilment, if I may call it, of all kinds were carried on, swearing or profane language was almost unknown, certainly unheard within the walls. Every auld callant must have noticed how strange that kind of language seemed to his ear, when he left the care of "Geordie" and had to mingle with outside companions.

Well, to resume, "Puddock" remarked that he would "draw the badger" if all would assist; and as the spirit of fun was on, "agreed" came from every side. Putting the gas down very low, each one being in bed, he proceeded to the ward door. Opening it, he knocked loudly at "Saum'l's" door. There was no response. Coming back into the ward, he placed a stool in a favourable spot, and proceeding to the door, knocked again. A skirling came from the inside.

"As sure as fate I'll report you," said the voice.

"No, you winna now, 'Saum'l'; you couldna for laughing"; then another knock or two.

Applying his mouth to the keyhole, "Puddock" cried in, "Aye, 'Saum'l,' whae gied the cook's cat ginger!"

This was a touchy point, carrying a smack of truth with it. It was too much for the stalwart wifie, who now sprang from her seat, and opening the door came on as fast as she could up the steps and into the ward, armed with a broomstick, after the retreating "chalker" of "The Puddock." He knew where the stool was; "Saum'l" did not, and over she went. This was the signal. Up jumped all the knaps; and if ever a wifie was "bowstered," "Saum'l" was. Soon she was crying for mercy, and when the knaps desisted she made a hasty retreat. Unfortunately, she was so bewildered as to take the washing-house door for the ward one, which was shut by the knaps. When she came to realise her position, she first demanded, then implored, then laughed at her position, and finally was released upon promising to say nothing about it. After she had gone, the gas was turned up and the fun re-

THE FIRST OR GOVIES' WARD.

commenced. Two contingents were battering at one another, when all of a sudden the end of one of the pillows split, and a cloud of down and feathers went flying from one end of the room to the other, leaving " Puddock " standing with, as he put it, " naething but a skinny, ill-fed rag in his hand." At this point the scene was changed to one of energetic industry; everyone was on his knees scraping together as many of the stray feathers as he possibly could.

A string tied round the mouth of the bag kept all secure until "Samm'l" could be coaxed to sew it up in the morning.

Another good joke of "Puddock's" was to carefully lift a tall boy's clothes and change them on his stool for those of a short one. In the morning of course this created great amusement. Sometimes, when most of the boys were asleep, a boy would be lifted bodily, mattress and everything. Then a few active spirits, laying the first one lifted on the long table, would shift half of the ward from one bed to another. A boy going to his bed at one end of the ward at night, might wake in the morning to find he had been sleeping in a bed at the other end. Of course the other half of the boys were in "the know," as it took seven or eight to do the thing successfully.

At other times the "ball-stick" would be used for body ornamentation on some sound sleeper. Both landscape and portrait subjects in black and white were chosen, which always caused great merriment on the bath night.

An oft-resorted to and rather an uncomfortable game for the sleeper was "couping." Two or three would take hold of one side of the mattress and with "one, two, three," knap and all were on the floor, the knap waking in a state of sudden and unaccountable wonderment at his change of position, although some would still sleep on comfortably enough for a long time after they were put over.

Another trick that caused much fun and merriment was often played on a cold winter night when one felt inclined to creep into bed and lovingly take his knees into his arms, not daring to stretch himself and feel the icy coldness of the sheets. In the morning, when jumping out of bed, he found that someone had been accommodating enough to tie the ends of his "chalker" like a bag, which made him cut rather a curious figure on the floor until he was untied.

CHAPTER XVIII.

CRIGHTON had gone into the sixth section, and was instructed in all the branches of education which the Hospital curriculum afforded. It was the highest class with the exception of the "Hopefuls," who were mostly boys remaining extra time in the institution, preparing for College studies.

Old M'Glashan, the dancing-master, was dead, and the class was not taken up that year. "Sprat" had retired from his situation as wardsman, amidst the cheers and hootings of the boys from their ward windows on the morning on which he removed his baggage. He left behind him three very reasonable fellows, John, Ja-ra-pa, and Long Jamie.

Muscle Doo still glued away in his little workshop at the shed. The knaps used to say that he would take a ladder with him to mend a hole in the floor, and they had many other lively remarks of the kind about poor Muscle. Peter was always flourishing, like his wild rhubarb in the back garden of the 'coud greens, which had nearly poisoned two little fellows who mistook it for an edible. Robertson had come into possession of the new house at the shed, and "Clyde," the terrier, had got a new companion named "Nero," a beautiful Newfoundland dog, which was a great favourite with the boys. Levick was as majestic and as much of a moralist as ever. He had brought the "Wark" band to great perfection, now that it was under his sole charge. He was presented with a suit of handsome regimentals, the empty sword belt of which the knaps promised to fill with a "curdie" subscription when they were auld callants. (For fulfilment, see page 136.) A glimpse was still to be had of Auld School Jenny, the midnight shadow, after the school cleaning was done, vanishing in the morning's grey light as the knaps came from their wards. Meenie had retired, and one of the wilies, named Eliza, succeeded Maggie More, who had gone to America, carrying with her a handsome gold watch and chain presented by the boys as a mark of affection.

Mammie M'Donald had also said good-bye to her boys, and a new matron reigned in her stead. She was a young-looking woman, with a pleasant and affectionate manner, and the boys all seemed to take well to her. The teachers had not been changed: Bob was still resident master, occupying the small suite of rooms next the store.

Walter had been advanced to the first seat in the chapel box, as his companion had left at the last half. The new chum who came to assist him was a good singer, but had something peculiar about one of his eyes—arising from an accident when he was a child—which gained him the name of "Bucking Jock." He was rather a clever lad, and along with one or two others formed a dramatic society, which was kindly taken charge of by "Bob," and brought to fair perfection, taking into account the slender resources and the few necessary properties which they had.

The company comprised Sinclair; Smith, acting manager; Lee, old-man; Tiger, principal lady; Loger, second lady;

Tarra, low comedian; Rhine, the heavy man and principal tragedian; and Walter, who occupied the position of stage manager. There were always plenty of extra hands when required, as well as an abundance of supers.

The properties were bought at Barney Barker's in the Cowgate, along with a large pair of light chintz curtains, to be used in lieu of scenery. The drop-scene was procured from Mammie, who gave the loan of a double set of marone repp window curtains, and promised to supply dresses for the ladies if she possibly could.

On different occasions they had played "The Streets of London," "Rob Roy," &c., winding up with some pantomime business. A drama entitled "The Rose of Ettrick Vale," to be preceded by the farce of "Box and Cox," was arranged for the first Friday night in December, the cast for which was— Box, Rhine; Cox, Crighton; with Tiger as Mrs Bouncer. For "The Rose of Ettrick Vale" it was as follows:

Red Ronald,	Rhine.
Old Adam,	Lee.
Albert,	Tiger.
Glenbrae,	Tarra.
Murdoch,	Ramsay.
Wandering Steenie,	Johnstone.
Guy o' the Gap,	Smith.
Black Wylie,	Sinclair.
Brand o' the Brae,	Crighton.
Laurette,	Loger.
Amy,	Wilson.
Jessie,	Grindlay.

Bob had the casting of the characters for both pieces, and he had apparently given all-round satisfaction.

His mind was set on having "Box and Cox" played with good effect, and two or three nights were spent with the hatter, printer, and parsimonious landlady in the "connie" of the seventh school, drilling them up in the many difficult colloquial parts of this clever farce.

After some difficulty he got them all up in their parts, and made them understand about their entrances and exits. The dresses were all in readiness, Mammie having supplied them for the ladies, and she also promised to dress them on the evening of the performance.

Some of the boys whose parents had old swords, pistols, or any odd weapon which would aid in adding to the ferocious appearance of the robber gang, obtained these for the occasion. The Thursday evening was to be a dress rehearsal, but the knaps found out that a certain amount of caution was necessary with those murderous-looking weapons.

The first accident occurred when one of the robbers (this was in the green or Cockie's wee room) proposed to try and split a book which Wilson held up on the point of a rapier. A grand slash was made at it with a hanger (said to have belonged to Robinson Crusoe), which missed the book and struck the knuckle of Wilson's finger. The wound was not very serious, but the practice called for caution.

The next mishap occurred in the first scene of the second act, at the grand encounter, and in which Brand fires a pistol at Old Adam. To make the affair more real, some powder was put into the pistol, although Bob's orders were that caps only should be used. The powder was sent home with paper, and plenty of it. The aim was true—too true for Lee, who nearly got his eyes put out; and his face kept smarting for a considerable time after the shot was fired. This put a stop to powder being used at all future plays.

Next afternoon, as soon as the arithmetic room was unoccupied, it was taken possession of by Muscle Doo and the Stage Committee, who straightway began work. The seats were all piled up on the east side of the room. A rope was stretched across, on which Mammie's curtains were run, after being stitched together so as to form two large curtains.

The chintz curtains belonging to the boys were then fixed along the back wall, with a passage crossing the stage behind the scenes. Several tables and covers were kept in the wings, to form rocks and other effects when required. The band boys were requested to supply the music. Mammie and the wifies had been asked to grace the company with their presence, as well as some friends who were visiting Dr Bedford.

The teachers and all officials in connection with the Hospital received "complimentaries," of which a number took advantage. After the "Hall," the boys hurried up, as no admittance could be permitted after the curtain rose, the audience having to come in by way of the stage.

All were in their places and a few pieces of music had been fairly well rendered by the band when the bell rang (a real bell this time). The curtains were drawn, and a murmur of astonishment and admiration at the wonderful effect ran through the audience.

The scene opened with the illustrious Cox scrutinizing his personal appearance in a small mirror, grumbling at his hairdresser for the shortness of the locks he had left on his scalp. The quaint humour, the startling points, and the ludicrous situations of this well-known farce were fairly well brought out, Tiger making a capital Mrs Bouncer; and as the curtain fell on the long-lost brothers, clasped in each other's arms, they received the genuine applause of the delighted spectators.

Another short selection of music, and again the bell tinkled. The curtains were drawn, with Bob ensconced as prompter at the R. L. E. The scene was made up of a farm-house, cottage, rustic bridge, and small stream. The surrounding country, rude and mountainous, was left to the imagination: but as Glenbrae spoke his opening lines, and sang his verses to gentle Jessie, the audience saw that the treat in store for them would well make up for the want of direct scenic effect.

The meeting between Glenbrae, Jessie, and Amy did cause a titter amongst the boys. When they heard Grindlay addressed as "my dearest Jessie" (this certainly was the weak point) even although Mammie's make-up was good, the very idea was too comical for the knaps.

All the characters were well up in their parts, and were closely watched by the prompter, who never failed when anything went wrong. "Guy o' the Gap" (Smith) was especially good, and the dialogue between Jessie, Guy, and Amy called forth loud applause. Wandering Steenie's quaint old border language and weird remarks were well spoken, and the bride was skilfully stolen away to the rugged fastnesses of Red Ronald.

Fights took place, accompanied with pistol shots and flashing swords; and the thunder and lightning representation was fairly well managed.

The third act opened in the Robbers' Cave, where several of the company were smuggled in. Some very amusing scenes took place with Guy and the thieves on guard. Towards the close, the identity of the bridegroom, Albert, is proved, by a poignard found on him when Old Adam took him from the arms of a stranger, and finally clinched by the confession of the repentant and dying Brand o' the Brae.

The arrival of the officers of justice and a band of armed soldiers put a stop to the free fighting, and all were subdued. Red Ronald sprang from the Bridge and perished in the torrent, and with the triumphant sentence of the faithful Steenie, the drama ended :—

"Shout, men o' Ettrick—
Shout for the Heir o' the Leonards
An' the Rose o' Ettrick Vale."

The "acting" in the School had developed in a most wonderful manner, and the elocution of the boys was really good when compared with the "Ha ha's" and "Ho Ho's" of former years.

Everyone was highly delighted with the exhibition; and the band playing "God save the Queen," the company dispersed. Bob gave the boys some encouragement by stating that they had far surpassed his expectations. He pointed out some improvements in tone of voice to some, in attitude to others, but upon the whole he thought it was "capital! capital!"

The Christmas holidays had passed, and Walter received his last Heriot cake and bun. "In another six weeks you will be home altogether" whispered his mother to him as he left for the "Wark" when his Christmas fortnight was over. Mary was leaving school now, and her sister, Kate, was still in the same situation.

When the first day or two was over, the lawds had settled down to study hard for their examination, which would take place a week earlier than the general one. English, French, Latin, Drawing, Writing, Arithmetic, Geography, Music, and Drill were the principal subjects in which they were expected to pass creditably, so that they had not much spare time to themselves.

One night a whisper went abroad that two of the knaps had skirted to see the pantomime — "Nanny" and the "Wee-Buck."

"Well," said one, "if they stop to the last, they canna be in before eleven, and the pend gate will be shut."

On going up to the wards, sure enough the two indicated were absent. Hurrying off to bed as fast as possible, the boys smuggled two extra pillows, and laying them under the bed-clothes with the supposed heads resting on the pillow, they made it appear as if the real occupants were quietly sleeping. Next, one gave his trousers, another a vest, and others jackets and boots, which were placed on the stools at the foot of the bedsteads; and, with a cap hung on the knob, he would have been a 'cute wardsman to detect anything wrong.

You may blame the boys, and rank them as participators for doing this, but the golden rule of "Do unto others as ye would have them do to you" was strong in the "Wark," and after all it was only fun.

The wardsman coming in gave a glance round the room, and satisfied himself that all was right. Walking round he turned down the lights, went out and locked the door taking the key into his own place. This was in the second ward.

But to follow the boys who had bolted. They were far from being bad or ill-intentioned lads. "Nanny" was a harum-scarum chap, ready for any amount of nonsense, never stopping to consider the consequences. The other had the character of an out-and-out Herioter.

"Nanny" had been out a message, and meeting with an auld callant, who used to be known by the name of "The Boar," he promised that if they would meet him in the Grassmarket that night he would take them to the Theatre Royal to see the pantomime. The offer was accepted, and so the three animals, "Boar," "Goat," and "Buck," had gallery seats as spectators of "Dick Whittington."

After it was over, all the three came up as far as the Heriot Bridge, where "The Boar" left. By this time it would be about half-past eleven, and it was only when they regained the greens that the serious nature of the situation struck them. They need not try the pend gate which they knew would be locked; so cutting through the 'ird greens they tried the parlour windows.

"This one comes down from the top," said "Nanny." It certainly did, but only so far as would admit his arm, not his head; even if it had, his body was to follow. Several plans were suggested, but nothing would work. At last they remembered that the 'cond school windows came down from the top, and that they could easily climb over the top if the window could only be reached. Stealing round, and examining as well as the darkness would permit, they concluded that the line of scalloped carving on the "connie" could be climbed if done cautiously. "Nanny" had often gone up so far, but never very high. However, they must try now. If once the millar were reached, the rest, they thought, would not be so "birsy."

"Nanny" was the first to try. Catching hold of the stone, which projected about three-quarters-of-an-inch on each side and formed a kind of ladder, he commenced the ascent. Up he went, clinging like a fly to the wall, by the points of fingers and toes. Steadily up, up until the millar was reached. Still he mounted upwards, and as his feet rested on the narrow ledge he stopped. The 'ist millar had about four inches of projection. With his face to the wall, and spreading out his arms, which gave him the appearance of a cross, he moved slowly along, inch by inch, pressing himself against the wall, and having about seven feet to traverse in this way. On reaching the inside "connie" or angle, he clutched the rain-water pipe which comes from the barty, and had a short rest.

Again he moved on, this time towards the 'cond school window, having five or six feet still further to go before his journey was completed. Reaching the window he tried it, and found that it came down nearly eighteen inches, and lifted an inch or two from the bottom as well. Whispering down to White to climb up on the window on the ground floor and scramble up the tirlies, he grasped the under-sill of the window, and hung his legs down as far as possible. His legs were caught by the "Wee-Buck," who then climbed up, and both landed on the window-ledge. Soon they were over the sash and sitting on one of the forms, considering what next to do.

Of course, they knew that the ward door would be locked, and that they need not try it; but they thought that perhaps the writing-school would not be closed. Upstairs, accordingly, they went, carrying their boots under their arms. All was darkness and silence.

The two "skirters" hardly breathed ; even the beating of their own hearts seemed to frighten them. Pulling open the double door of the 'coml school, they gently closed the creaking hoist arrangement, as it now appeared to them, shutting their teeth hard together as if that would help the care with which they were closing the doors inch by inch. At last they were shut, and a long breath was drawn as if some danger were past. Stealing out they made to mount the stairs which took them to the writing-school. It was only a few yards distant, and as they reached the steps they distinctly heard a half-stifled cough. They paused and crouched down in terror on the steps.

"What's that?" whispered "Nanny," quickly.

Perhaps it struck them at the moment that the drummer's step was near. Could it be his ghost? No; the sound seemed to come from behind. From the passage through which they had just passed a soft and cautious step was heard approaching. The "Wee-Buck" clung to "Nanny's" arm, the cold sweat breaking out upon both.

In the direction of the "Bells" door they saw a pair of glaring eyes, as if some demon from the realms below had followed them, and now appeared to raise accusation against them. Still stared those balls of phosphorus, which riveted the terror-stricken evil-doers.

Slowly the ghastly orbs moved forward until a sudden movement of "Nanny" startled the goblin and it made a bound past them.

It was only the cook's cat, which had been mousing in Fummie's bunker! A moment's mental and physical rest brought them round, when they congratulated each other and cursed the cat.

With extra caution they again mounted the stair. Joy! the writing-school door was unlocked. Entering, they hastily closed it behind them, took a seat, and proceeded to hatch further plans.

"Nanny's" first remark was: "I ken it's John that rings the bell in the morning, so when we hear him gann out we'll pop in."

This being agreed to, they repaired to Fuffie's desk and, getting under the knee-hole, they sat and told stories to keep themselves awake. About twenty minutes to six they heard the ward door open and, as John's footsteps died away downstairs, they got out and into the ward.

Hastening towards their beds, they cast off their already loosened clothing, and soon were innocently lying on their separate couches, to the great astonishment of the knaps when the bell rang.

This escapade was never found out, and was possibly the most daring thing of the kind that ever passed undetected in the school.

CHAPTER XIX.

AS was the usual custom, the lawds had been invited to tea with Mammie, and it passed off splendidly. Walter and five more of the boys were to sing at the apprentices' soiree and concert to be held in Heriot Bridge School. All the auld callant apprentices were invited to this annual gathering, and a noble spread of tea, cake, and fruit was laid before them. Songs and music were provided, and on the whole a very pleasant evening was spent.

Thursday next was the lawds' examination; and to-morrow being Saturday Walter and one or two others were going to Tibbets in the South Bridge to select a "rounder" instead of the usual "balmoral;" also to procure a "dickie," collar, and tie, which was as necessary for the lawds' examination as fig-cake and cocoa-nuts were for the excursion. When they came in on Saturday night, all the lawds were gathered together comparing notes. "Tobs" and ties there were in abundance—the latter generally of a high colour, tartan being greatly in favour.

The lawds' examination came at last. Each was dressed in his new out-going tweed suit. Proud indeed they were, especially of the side-pockets in the trousers, out of which it was an impossibility to keep the hands. Each one became the centre of a little group of admiring knaps, who with wistful glances eyed the lawds and wished, both aloud and in silence, that they were leaving too.

"Only six months," one would say.

"An' I've got two years," another would remark, with a shrug of the shoulders.

The bell rang for the outgoing boys to appear in the council-room. On entering each one seated himself in front of an ink bottle, a pen, and paper, which were laid on tables round the room. The examiners, taking their seats, dictated questions, and each boy wrote the answer on his paper. This done, the papers were signed and collected, and a short oral examination followed. A sum was worked out by each on the black board; and, finally, one of them, in the space of a few seconds, drew the map of England very correctly, with the principal towns, rivers, and mountains, receiving great praise from the Govies for his skill. At one o'clock a *paté* was given for dinner to all the boys; and what was more they had a half-holiday.

On Sunday the lawds went to Greyfriars Church for the last time as knaps, casting long looks at the tombstones and well-known mounds on the way. There were "Geordie's table" and "chair"—two trees trimmed in the shape of those articles of furniture. They were named "Geordie's" by the boys.

Reaching the corner of the church, they looked, perhaps for the last time, at those oft-read and never-to-be-forgotten lines, which are carved on a tablet placed against the south-west corner of the church and in memory of Allan Ramsay, the first stanza of which runs:

> "Though here you're buried, worthy Allan,
> We'll ne'er forget you, canty callan':
> For while your soul lives in the sky,
> Your 'Gentle Shepherd' ne'er can die."

Passing on and into church they listened to a sermon from the worthy pastor, Dr Robertson.

The afternoon was spent by the lawds walking about arm in arm, talking over their future prospects. Some had situations to enter upon at once; others were to leave town for their homes at a distance; and a few had not yet decided upon any employment.

It was imperative that they should get a situation as an indentured apprentice soon, so as to ensure them getting their "maiks," as they termed the £50 received by each boy boy who finished his bound apprenticeship.

During the following week, the Doctor requested the company of the out-going boys to tea at his apartments. He and his good lady talked very kindly to them, instructing them in many little points of table etiquette, which had more purpose than the knaps then thought, falling as it did on virgin ground, ripe to receive it after many years of long-table dining.

On Wednesday night it was with very mixed feelings that the lawds went to bed in the Govies' ward. The truth, think as they liked, could not be realised; but it was the last night in the "Wark." The little single beds on which they rested so long and so comfortably, after this night would know them no more. In a few hours all would be past of the Garring law for them, and a new set would take the honoured position.

The next sleep would be on a different pillow—perhaps a better, perhaps one not so good. They might be going to homes with loving parents wishing for and patiently waiting their return; or maybe they were going out only to burden some relations who had enough to do with themselves. With thoughts such as these they fell asleep.

George Heriot's Hospital.

In the morning great preparations went on with the dressing. They had two suits of clothes—one black doeskin and the other of a grey material. On the bed were laid the outfit and articles which they were to take home: half-a-dozen shirts, two night shirts or "chalkers," half-a-dozen

LEAVING THE "WARK"

pairs of socks, some handkerchiefs, white and coloured, braces, ties and collars, gloves, &c., brushes and comb, and other articles of a like kind.

For books there were a handsome pocket Bible in a black morocco binding, a Scripture handbook, a "Youth's

Companion," an arithmetical treatise, a dictionary, and a copy of the history of the "Wark" by Dr Stephens.

The dressing in the doeskins or blacks was carried on amidst great clamour, several of the "cholds" and companions of the would-be swells coming in to assist in the operation. The fixing of collars and ties was altogether out of the province of a Herioter, all the regulation linen of that kind being fixed to the shirts.

And who ever felt himself so great a swell as an auld callant during the first hour of his new being, new life—the realisation of a long dream? Shoulders square, head well elevated, rounder tipped to the side, tartan scarf of bright shade neatly tied. If he should be fortunate enough to have a watch, more than likely it would be in the wrong pocket. Nevertheless, don't forget he was somebody, and somebody of consequence; in fact, to the small boys a person of great importance—*was he not about to leave the " Wark!"*

When their toilet was completed, they went downstairs and the classes commenced; numbers of friends and visitors gathered and followed the boys round the various rooms. Between twelve and one o'clock the exercise of drill was engaged in, the lawds handling for the last time the carbines they were so proud of. That done, and the dinner over in the hall, all repaired to the Seventh school or Lecture room, where the silver medal was to be presented to the boy whose behaviour and ability had been the best.

A speech was delivered by one of our great and respected friends amongst the Govies. He was a Magistrate with a name which entirely belied his character, and whose timely and welcome appearance in our class-rooms oft saved us from punishment—John Tawse. He gave us a parting advice

BAILIE JOHN TAWSE.

which if followed would certainly lead to everything that was good.

The Doctor then bade the lawds, as it were, good-bye. His remarks were, to say the least, very touching. He seemed to have a fund of love for every boy who came under his charge, and always felt keenly when they had to leave.

"My dear boys," he said, with a touch of sadness in his voice, "whatever you do, be truthful, manly, and just, in whatever position you may be placed, and I have no doubt if you follow the example we have put before you, and the lessons we have tried to teach you, you will turn out wise, happy, and prosperous men. Be an honour to yourselves, and a credit to the institution in which you have passed so many of your boyhood's years."

On leaving the room they went to the ward, and secured the big, bulky, black bag which contained their " providing." Our friend, Walter, had divided his into parcels, of which his mother and sisters each carried a share ; and to the tones of the "Wark" bell he now took his way, as it were, out into the world, for better or for worse.

CHAPTER XX.

MANY years have elapsed since Walter left the Hospital. Like most auld callants he has had his share of the ups and downs of life. Having secured an appointment under the Indian Government, he proceeded from his situation in London to Calcutta.

At last his turn of leave of absence came, and gladly he made tracks for the Old Country.

What his thoughts were, as he looked once more, from the window of the Flying Scotsman, on the lion guarding the city which he had so longed to see again—his old home—and again when he stepped on to the Waverley platform and afterwards into Princes Street, can be better imagined than described.

A few days after his arrival a strong desire took possession of him to visit the scenes of his boyhood. As he made for the centre of these, he realised with feelings of regret the changes that time had wrought. Many places were still the same; but others, to which he could have gone blindfold, had been cleared away.

But this is June Day and he must be on to the dear old "Wark" to join once more in the festivities and sing again the old songs; to wander through its well-remembered connies and rooms, and maybe meet some of his old chums. Then some scudding—and then—

Arrived at the Lauriston gate, he was boldly walking into the grounds when an open hand was held out to him. Walter was about to grasp it with a hearty shake, when a manly voice demanded his *ticket*.

"A what? Ticket, did you say? I beg your pardon, there must be some mistake. I am an auld callant." This information was given with chest out and head well elevated.

"I canna help it, ma man; auld or young callant, if you hivna a ticket ye canna get in."

Walter staggered back at this chilling reception, but an auld callant coming forward and hearing the latter part of Walter's conversation with the gate-keeper and noting the difficulty, produced an extra card of admission, and with a friendly grip of the hand the two old scholars passed together slowly up the approach.

Taking a long look at the stately pile, Walter saw no outward change on it—just the same; every stone, even many of the chips in the balusters, he knew, and they seemed to speak a welcome to him. They strolled round to the square to see the buskin'—what! not a flower!

"Why are none of the auld callants up scudding?" asked Walter.

"Oh," said his friend, "we could not scud now; there are no tirlies on the windows:" and he might have added that, with a new order of things, ball-making was a lost art.

Walter, sick at heart with disappointment at those (to him) terribly vital changes, allowed his thoughts to run back to the days o' auld lang syne. He was awakened from his reverie by colliding with a janitor on his way to the Council Room.

"I should know that face," said Walter—"Oh, yes"—

"How are you, William—you are William Duncan?"

"Yes, but you have the best of me," was the reply.

There he was, with just the same pleasant smile and cheering word; and Walter felt it refreshing indeed amidst the changes around him.

"Don't you remember me?—Walter Crighton."

"Oh, yes, I remember you quite well now when you speak : but of course I was after your time."

"A few changes in the inside here," said Walter.

"Yes, you will hardly know the old place now."

After a moment or two's chat, William passed on, and Walter and his friend resumed their look round.

Going over to the Lodge they had a look in and found it much the same. An amusing incident occurred here : each discovered the other rubbing his hands in a manner very suggestive of an impending thrashing, and looking round for the board where the bad marks used to be shown, the force of habit being apparently very strong.

They next went to see that sacred and historical apartment, "The Buffie." It was altered — quite a gorgeous place, with no space for a "set-to."

On they wandered; but what changes—no parlours, no bolls, no bedrooms, no kitchen, no hall. Yes, the hall was still there, with a pastry shop at one end of it, and a few of the same old tables. Walter looked underneath one of them and noticed with satisfaction that the little cleeks and shelves had not been removed. On the walls the boards still hung with names of the former medallists written in letters of gold.

Quietly, hat in hand, and with deep feelings of reverence they stood once more within the Chapel. A great alteration had been made on it. To the ordinary visitor little would be noticed, but the feelings within the breasts of Walter and his friend were too deep for words. Scenes grave and gay enacted within its sacred precincts passed through their minds. "Abide with me"—Walter fancied he could hear the music of that beautiful hymn softly stealing out from what was left of the carvings of the pulpit. The pulpit— once the knaps' pride, said to be the loftiest in our fair city and now cut almost in halves—stood like a giant with his limbs cut off and set down on the stumps, all its stately look gone. How majestic it used to be, how almost sad a sight it was now. "Come on!"

They left the Chapel and passed through the pend gate to the 'ird greens. Quite a crowd had gathered to witness the games—to the auld callant a poor substitute for the old time June Day celebrations.

Walter took a general survey of his surroundings. The beautiful shrubbery and green lawn had disappeared; there was no turning-house, no Governor's garden—all had been removed, and the ground was laid out as a large flat gravel-covered playground. Heriot Bridge School building was still there, with many additions, and was utilised for mechanical class-rooms, Swimming Bath, &c., in connection with the institution. Truly, the old cistern had "*grow'd.*"

On the ground of the auld wife's garden, where flourished the grand old pear-tree, now stood a huge red-brick building, evidently a brewery.

"Who are all these little fellows in the white knicker suits?" asked Walter.

"Oh, they are the knaps of to-day," answered his friend, "and instead of 180 there are over 900 of them."

"Where do they find accommodation for the teaching of such a number of boys." asked Walter.

"Oh," said his friend, "most of the wards, library, and many other places have been turned into class-rooms, and there is a greatly increased teaching staff—grand men they are, and mostly members of the Heriot Club."

Games of all kinds were in progress and being keenly contested in quite a business-like fashion. What a contrast to the sunny green, merry laughter, and humble romps of the June Day of long ago.

"Do none of the boys live in the Wark?" asked Walter, again.

"Oh, no," remarked his friend. "At six o'clock the pend gate is locked, and all are away by that time, out to their homes."

Poor old "Wark"! How different to what it used to be when your noisy nurslings caressed your corners and pillars as they merrily played at the various games of "tig" till their weary limbs or the sound of the evening bell made them lie down to rest under your folding care.

"There is certainly a great change in everything here," remarked Walter's friend, "but possibly it is for the better."

"Maybe—maybe," was Walter's reply, for still his conservative spirit felt it should have been left the same as of yore.

Walter was met and welcomed by several of his former chums, and as they strolled together towards the town by the way of Greyfriars' gate, they had many a laugh over the stories recounted and added to by one and another of the company.

Walter asked many questions about his old play-fellows.

"What about Tom Ross? what did he follow after?"

"Oh, he went into the engineering trade and is now abroad somewhere," answered his friend; "Sinclair and Johnstone are away out of town. In fact, Johnstone, if I am not mistaken, is in London, and making a big thing of it."

"A big thing of London do you mean?" pawkily asked the Rev. Thomas Mice.

A good hearty laugh followed the reverend gentleman's remark.

"No, no; he is in the dog collar line, and if you care to wire up to him he may be able to get you a few cheap," retorted Walter's guide.

"And Taylor," asked Walter; "where is he?"

"Also in London," said Greig; "and Smith — you remember Smith — he has the management of a large banking establishment in Paris. For the rest — Tod is a commercial, and a number of our set went for doctors, ministers, and lawyers; but if you come to the dinner to-night you will meet quite a number of auld callants— before, during, and after our time."

Before parting at the gate, they all arranged to meet at the "Auld Callants' Dinner" of the "Heriot Club," in the evening.

Arriving in good time at the hotel in which the dinner was to be held, Walter met many of his old school-fellows, and was very much struck with the absence of all that class distinction so noticeable in gatherings of a similar kind: the physician, the teacher, the well-to-do merchant, the mechanic, all bound together by the common brotherhood, conversed and chaffed with each other in such a friendly and hearty manner: callants of all periods from and before the "thirties" up to the present time, presided over by a genial and enthusiastic old knap, with men of similar spirit as supporters. The hours soon sped: the loyal and patriotic toasts having been duly honoured, the toast of the evening, "The Immortal Memory of George Heriot," proposed by the chairman, whose words found an echo in the breasts of all present, was pledged, followed by the song, "The Merry Month of June." That song went with a heartiness which Walter had never heard before—such a volume of sound, and the words expressed so energetically conveyed their full meaning. Gentlemen were in the company who had possibly never sang a stave since boyhood, but they were at it with a will now.

As the evening proceeded, telegrams were read from auld knaps resident in far-off lands. These were greeted with cheers, some remarks being passed relating to the senders, and the company felt as if they were the centre of that great band of Auld Callants, so widely scattered over both hemispheres but all joining with one accord, congratulating one another and entering heartily in the celebrations of the natal day of the generous founder of that noble Hospital which had been such a boon to all its sons.

Stories from callants and teachers—not omitting the one old friend, Mr ———, still as full of quaint, curious, and instructive anecdote, and who made the speech of the evening, part of his remarks being to this effect, "Gentlemen, we are here to cherish a glorious past, and to us the glorious past is our schoolboy days—great days and great deeds; how when we used to jump the walls, how we outdid the French master, how we ran away from school and got punished for it, &c. Those are the days of days—the days that our minds love to go back upon and cherish, the recollection of which helps us to go along through life and fight out our worries of manhood."

Songs from others of well-known names — songs with choruses in which we all joined; and thus the evening was spent bringing vividly to our remembrance those happy days—

> "When we were boys, merry, merry boys,
> When we were boys together;
> It seems to me but yesterday
> Since we were boys together."

GLOSSARY.

These words were used invariably by the boys in the Hospital. To substitute any other expression was enough to put any boy out of caste.

Bakes—Biscuits.
Ball—Boot Blacking.
Barty (Bartizan)—Battlement, tower.
Bat—To Fight.
Bawser—One who speaks with a bass voice.
Bells, The—A store where the repaired clothing was kept.
Birse—Anger, passion.
Birsy—Difficult, angry.
Bist—A Football.
Blazing—Bragging, swaggering, showing off.
Blobs—Gooseberries or other berries.
Bolls—The boys' wardrobe.
Bolt—Run. *To Bolt*—To run away from the school intending never to return.
Bouch—To spoil.
Boukie Sumph—Squinting fool.
Bowster—A pillow.
Brat—Skin of porridge.
Bree—Hurry; to spring past.
Buck—To squint.
Buddy—Scabbed.
Buffie—Fighting apartment.
Bug—Name given to "knaps" by the "nests."

Bume—To throw; to throw a ball or stone high in the air.
Bulsher—A playing marble.
Bun—Cake.
Butt—Butter.

Cadge—To beg.
Caikie—Daft, silly.
Cap—To seize by violence.
Cawrie—Soft part of bread.
Chaps—To choose.
Chat—Impudence.
Chave—To tease, to cause a desire for, to tempt.
Chalker—Long white night-shirt.
Chip-in—To feast.
Chit—Bread.
Chizzy—Chosen spoon of a garrier.
Chodd—A boy who had twelve months to complete in the Hospital.
Chucks—Knots of meal in porridge.
Chums a'—Friends all.
Cleek—To keep watch for the coming of the one in charge.
Cliff—A sharp stroke with the open hand.
Cod—To make believe.

Glossary

'Cond—Second.
Cone—Beef.
Connie—Corner.
Cout—String with knotted end.
Cricks—Pieces of illustrated journals having pictures.
Crockle—Crust of bread.
Crowning—A boy's birthday celebrations.
Cude—Butler, store-keeper.
Cude's Wash—Small beer.
Curdie—A farthing.
Cutty—A spoon.

Dakie—A crow.
Dantie—A friend to one of the bigger boys.
Daverer—A shuffler, a bad payer.
Dibs—Pay, salary.
Dift—Bad stotting ball.
Dirk—To spoil, to bungle.
Doddie—One who scraped trash together.
Dollop—A large quantity (of anything).
Doliker—A large playing marble.
Don—Dux in class. *A Don*—One who was good in any class or at sport.
Dose—Small loaf of bread.
Douchie—Bottom of class. *A Douchie*—Not clever at lessons.
Douf—To fix out of reach by throwing.

Ess—To save.

Fan—Small loaf of bread with crust on top, bottom, and side.
Flapit—Splay-footed.
Flee-on—A command to seize.
Flap—Boy of clumsy appearance.

Fud—Afraid.
Fum—Disagreeable smell.

Gab—Impertinence.
Garr—The best boxer in the school.
Garrier—(Old name) same as lawd.
Gess—To play truant.
Gib—Gundy, candy.
Giny—Dirt, mud.
Gocie—Governor.
Gun and Sword—Seed-cake and shortbread.
Gush—Sorrow, pity.

Hain—To save, to gather up.
Half-dose—Half-portion of bread.
Hashy quarter—The three months before June Day.
Hawker—One who was not a Herioter, an outsider.
Hokie—Punishment given on a particular part.
Hough—Fat of beef.

'Ird—Third.
'Ist—First.

Jaw—To give impudence.
Judy—Sweetheart.

Katie-Flips—Three-cornered sugar sweets.
Kecker—Black eye, from a blow.
Keelie—Ragged bad character.
Kell—Ringworm.
Kemp—To sup hurriedly.
Kid—Boy first six months at school. *To kid*—To deceive.
Kiddie—A candle.
Knap—General name for all boys in school.

Lambing—Skating well and artistically.
Laird—Boy's title during his last six months in School.
Leads—The lead roof of the Hospital Buildings.
Lip—Impertinence.

Maiks—Money.
Mammie—The matron of Hospital.
Mauk—To feign illness.
Mealie—A mob.
Meiser—A hoarder, a greedy boy.
Mellin'—Thrashing.
Millars—Ledges on building.
Muckle Chields—Seven eldest boys (old).
Muggin'—A thrashing.

Nab—Petty theft.
Nacket—A little ball.
Nac—To strike smartly.
Nay—No.
Neet—Boy of George Watson's Hospital.
Nits—Nuts.
Nugget—A thick-headed boy.

Palie—Sweet, delicious.
Paste—To strike.
Pátés—Pies.
Pay-in—To give in charity, to subscribe.
Pea-claw—Pea soup.
Pianin'—Thrashing.
Pint—Boot-lace.
Plout—A poker.
Plum-pud—Plum pudding.
Pena—Task in very small writing, a punishment.
Porter—Wardsman.
Pot—Porridge.

Prap—A target.
Priman—Prize-book.
Prodie—A trinket, toy, or any curiosity.
Properties—Woodwork used in the June Day decorations.

Rorie—A lie.
Roux—To win all a boy's marbles from him.

S—s—(Hissing sound) to give alarm, sign of danger.
Scaa—Scabbed.
Scadge—Ask for.
Scour—Spoil a game; to frighten.
Scogie—Fag, servant.
Scrimp—Mean, narrow.
Scuddie—A punishing order given by a lawd.
Scudding—Hitting.
Sel'—Beware (same as S—S).
Shie—Throw for.
Shovelie—Fireman.
Skeeh—To ask often and from all.
Skin—To steal from a boy.
Skin Doses—A snatching order given by a lawd.
Skirt—To run out of the Hospital.
Skit—To steal.
Smood—To crawl; go quietly.
Snitch—To tell.
Sock—Sweetmeats of any kind.
Specie—An example of writing, &c.
Spurr—Hurry.
Squeeze Pouches—An order given by a lawd to crush pockets.
Stabido—(stappit-nose) one who speaks with a nasal twang.
Sumph—A stupid fellow.

Swad—A soldier.
Swags—Pockets.
Sweir—Reluctant, unwilling to part with.
Sweired soul—Unwilling person.
Swipie—A loose game at cricket.
Sword and Gun—Bun and Shortbread.
Swypes—Beer (penny)
Sye—Sixpence.

Taw—A game at marbles.
Taws—Fun.
Tawnie—Bully, a boy who was continually flogging the smaller ones.
Thrym—Threepence.
Tirlies—Wire-netting covers on windows.
Tob—Round hat.
Toll-out—Deliver up.
Touts—Potatoes.

Trash—Odds and ends of all and sundry curiosities. (Some pieces of trash were always about the place and were bought and exchanged, just as the antiquarian does with his relics. The possession of certain well-known pieces brought their possessors into note in our Commonwealth.)
Tym—Twopence.
Vacance—Holiday time.
Wark—The Hospital.
Wifie—Maid-servant.
Willies—Clippings of cloth, tailor's rinds.
Yochie—Highlander, kiltie.
Yake—Yes.
Yaps—Apples.

The above words are derived from old Scots, French, Latin, and other languages. Very few of the Scots words were used in the *pure* either in pronunciation or meaning, but nearly all had a particular twang and interpretation which was religiously observed and handed down from generation to generation by the inhabitants of this miniature kingdom in the heart of a great city. With the domestic changes of recent years, these words have gradually been slipping away, and have now almost disappeared.

www.ingramcontent.com/pod-product-compliance
Lightning Source LLC
Chambersburg PA
CBHW022106230426
43672CB00008B/1299